THE EXPANDING CYBER THREAT

HEARING

BEFORE THE

SUBCOMMITTEE ON RESEARCH AND TECHNOLOGY

COMMITTEE ON SCIENCE, SPACE, AND TECHNOLOGY

HOUSE OF REPRESENTATIVES

ONE HUNDRED FOURTEENTH CONGRESS

FIRST SESSION

JANUARY 27, 2015

Serial No. 114–2

Printed for the use of the Committee on Science, Space, and Technology

Available via the World Wide Web: http://science.house.gov

U.S. GOVERNMENT PUBLISHING OFFICE

93–880PDF WASHINGTON : 2015

For sale by the Superintendent of Documents, U.S. Government Publishing Office
Internet: bookstore.gpo.gov Phone: toll free (866) 512–1800; DC area (202) 512–1800
Fax: (202) 512–2104 Mail: Stop IDCC, Washington, DC 20402–0001

CONTENTS

January 27, 2015

IV

THE EXPANDING CYBER THREAT

TUESDAY, JANUARY 27, 2015

HOUSE OF REPRESENTATIVES,
SUBCOMMITTEE ON RESEARCH AND TECHNOLOGY
COMMITTEE ON SCIENCE, SPACE, AND TECHNOLOGY,
Washington, D.C.

The Subcommittee met, pursuant to call, at 2:03 p.m., in Room 2318 of the Rayburn House Office Building, Hon. Barbara Comstock [Chairwoman of the Subcommittee] presiding.

Congress of the United States
House of Representatives
COMMITTEE ON SCIENCE, SPACE, AND TECHNOLOGY

2321 RAYBURN HOUSE OFFICE BUILDING

WASHINGTON, DC 20515–6301

(202) 225–6371
www.science.house.gov

Subcommittee on Research and Technology

The Expanding Cyber Threat

Tuesday, January 27, 2015
2:00 p.m. to 4:00 p.m.
2318 Rayburn House Office Building

Witnesses

Ms. Cheri McGuire, *Vice President, Global Government Affairs & Cybersecurity Policy, Symantec Corporation*

Dr. James Kurose, *Assistant Director, Computer and Information Science and Engineering (CISE) Directorate, National Science Foundation*

Dr. Charles H. Romine, *Director, Information Technology Laboratory, National Institute of Standards and Technology*

Dr. Eric A. Fischer, *Senior Specialist in Science and Technology, Congressional Research Service*

Mr. Dean Garfield, *President and CEO, Information Technology Industry Council*

U.S. HOUSE OF REPRESENTATIVES
COMMITTEE ON SCIENCE, SPACE, AND TECHNOLOGY
SUBCOMMITTEE ON RESEARCH AND TECHNOLOGY

The Expanding Cyber Threat

Tuesday, January 27, 2015
2:00 p.m. – 4:00 p.m.
2318 Rayburn House Office Building

Purpose

On Tuesday, January 27, 2015, the Research and Technology Subcommittee will hear from private sector and government experts about issues related to cybersecurity, including impacts to critical infrastructure, cyber hardware and software, and personal security and privacy stemming from cyber threats, attacks and breaches in order to inform the Committee's legislative work. The Committee's jurisdiction includes research and development related to cybersecurity at the National Science Foundation (NSF), the National Institute of Standards and Technology (NIST), and the Department of Homeland Security's Science and Technology Directorate (DHS S&T).

Witnesses

- **Ms. Cheri McGuire**, Vice President, Global Government Affairs & Cybersecurity Policy, Symantec Corporation
- **Dr. James Kurose**, Assistant Director, Computer and Information Science and Engineering (CISE) Directorate, National Science Foundation.
- **Dr. Charles H. Romine**, Director, Information Technology Laboratory, National Institute of Standards and Technology
- **Dr. Eric A. Fischer**, Senior Specialist in Science and Technology, Congressional Research Service
- **Mr. Dean Garfield**, President and CEO, Information Technology Industry Council

Overview

Information technology (IT) is continuously evolving, leading to markedly increased connectivity and productivity for industry, government and personal use. The benefits provided by these advancements have led to the widespread use and incorporation of information technologies across major sectors of the economy. This level of connectivity and the dependence of our critical infrastructure systems on IT have also increased the vulnerability of these systems. Reports of cyber criminals, "hacktivists" and nation-states accessing sensitive information and disrupting services in both the public and private domains have risen steadily, heightening concerns over the adequacy of our cybersecurity measures.

Cybersecurity related concerns range from spearfishing attempts and spam, to malware, to illegal or illicit activity on the darknet (private networks using non-standard protocols not connected to the internet). More and more cases of successful cyber-attacks are being reported. Financial information, medical records, any and all personal data maintained on computer systems by individuals or by organizations large and small are vulnerable. Mobile, wireless technology presents new opportunities for cyber-attacks. As more devices communicate with one another, from security systems to thermostats, the "Internet of Things" presents a growing target. Social media sites and advertisements also present opportunities for cybersecurity breaches. A number of companies with cybersecurity services compile data and have made predictions about cyber threats. "[I]n 2014, Proofpoint found a 650% increase in social media spam compared to 2013."[1]

During the 113th Congress, the Science, Space, and Technology Committee held a number of hearings on issues related to cybersecurity including a February 2013 hearing, *Cybersecurity Research and Development: Challenges and Solutions*[2]; a January 2014 hearing, *Healthcare.gov: Consequences of Stolen Identity*[3]; and a March 2014 hearing, *Can Technology Protect Americans from International Cybercriminals.*[4] Each hearing explored a different aspect of cybersecurity concerns facing Americans today.

High-profile cyber breaches in recent months include: Target and Home Depot financial transaction systems, Apple's iCloud systems, Sony, and the U.S. Central Command. The number and changing nature of threats serves to underscore the importance of safeguarding information technology and systems.

According to the U.S. Government Accountability Office, "[f]ederal agencies have significant weaknesses in information security controls that continue to threaten the confidentiality, integrity, and availability of critical information and information systems used to support their operations, assets, and personnel."[5] In fiscal year 2014, the federal government spent more than $81 billion on information technology.[6] "Federal agencies spend a significant part of their annual IT funding on cybersecurity, which currently constitutes more than one in every eight dollars of agency IT budgets."[7]

Cybersecurity research and development efforts include working on the prevention of cyber-attacks, detecting attacks as they are occurring, responding to attacks effectively, mitigating severity, recovering quickly, and identifying responsible parties. Research and development provides a better understanding of weaknesses in systems and networks and of how to protect those systems and networks.

---

[1] http://www.proofpoint.com/threatinsight/posts/cybersecurity-predictions-for-2015.php
[2] http://science.house.gov/hearing/subcommittee-technology-and-subcommittee-research-joint-hearing-cyber-rd-challenges-and
[3] http://science.house.gov/hearing/full-committee-hearing-healthcaregov-consequences-stolen-identity
[4] http://science.house.gov/hearing/subcommittee-oversight-and-subcommittee-research-and-technology-joint-hearing-can-technology
[5] http://www.gao.gov/key_issues/cybersecurity/issue_summary#t=0
[6] http://www.whitehouse.gov/sites/default/files/omb/assets/egov_docs/omb_presidents_it_budget_for_fy_2015_summary_chart.pdf
[7] http://www.fas.org/sgp/crs/misc/R43831.pdf

The National Science Foundation

The National Science Foundation (NSF) is the principal agency supporting unclassified cybersecurity research and development as well as technical education. The NSF Directorate for Computer and Information Science and Engineering (CISE) promotes the progress of computer and information sciences, advances the development and use of cyberinfrastructure and leads the Foundation's Secure and Trustworthy Cyberspace investment to build a knowledge base in cybersecurity and a cyber-secure society. NSF has made investments in cybersecurity education and workforce. The Scholarship for Service program, recently codified in *The Cybersecurity Enhancement Act* (PL 113-274), provides awards to increase the number of students entering the computer security and information assurance fields, and to increase the capacity of institutions of higher education to produce professionals in these fields. NSF also offers Advanced Technological Education (ATE) grants educating technicians for high-technology fields with a focus on two-year colleges.

CISE was funded at $894 million in fiscal year 2014 (FY14), the President's budget request was just over $893 million for FY 15. Scholarship for Service received $45 million for FY14 and the FY15 request included $25 million. ATE funding levels of nearly $125 million in FY14 were maintained in the FY15 request.

The National Institute of Standards and Technology

The National Institute of Standards and Technology's (NIST) core cybersecurity focus areas include: research, development, and specification; secure system and component configuration; and assessment and assurance of security properties of products and systems. In 2014, NIST released the *Framework for Improving Critical Infrastructure Cybersecurity* stemming from a 2013 Executive Order (more details below). Title III of the E-Government Act (PL 107-347), the Federal Information Security Management Act of 2002 (FISMA), tasked NIST with developing cybersecurity standards, guidelines, and associated methods and techniques for use by the Federal Government. In April 2011, the Administration tasked NIST with leading the National Strategy for Trusted Identities in Cyberspace (NSTIC), an initiative focused on establishing identity solutions and privacy-enhancing technologies to improve the security and convenience of sensitive online transactions.

NIST's Information Technology Laboratory (ITL) leads the organization's cybersecurity related responsibilities. ITL is a part of NIST's six laboratory units under the Science and Technical Research Services (STRS) appropriations line item. In FY14 ITL was funded at over $109 million, the FY15 request was $111 million.

In December 2014, *The Cybersecurity Enhancement Act of 2015* (PL 113-274) passed the House and Senate and was signed into law. The new law strengthens the efforts of NSF and NIST in the areas of cybersecurity technical standards and cybersecurity awareness, education, and workforce development. PL 113-274 coordinates research and related activities conducted across the Federal agencies to better address evolving cyber threats.

The Department of Homeland Security Science and Technology Directorate

In fiscal year 2011, the DHS Science and Technology Directorate (S&T) established the Cyber Security Division (CSD) within S&T's Homeland Security Advanced Research Projects Agency (HSARPA). CSD works to enhance the security and resilience of the nation's critical information infrastructure and the Internet. CSD develops and delivers new technologies, tools and techniques to enable DHS and the U.S. to defend, mitigate and secure current and future systems, networks and infrastructure against cyber-attacks. CSD serves a wide range of customers and partners within DHS and at other federal agencies, state and municipal administrations and first responders, and private sector organizations.

In FY14 DHS S&T was funded at $1.2 billion, the FY15 request was nearly $1.1 billion for the Directorate. HSARPA and CSD fall under the Research, Development and Innovation line item for DHS S&T which in FY 14 was funded at $462 million and in FY15 the Administration requested nearly $434 million.

Executive Order on Improving Critical Infrastructure and Framework for Improving Critical Infrastructure Cybersecurity

In February 2013, President Obama issued an executive order (EO 13636) on cybersecurity for critical infrastructure.[8] Among other provisions, the EO encouraged information sharing between public and private sectors and directed NIST to lead the development of a framework to reduce cyber risks to critical infrastructure. NIST was instructed to work with industry to identify existing voluntary consensus standards and industry best practices to incorporate into the framework.

In February 2014, NIST released the *Framework for Improving Critical Infrastructure Cybersecurity* in response to the EO. NIST worked in collaboration with industry stakeholders to establish a three-pronged *Framework* that includes a Core, Profile and Implementation Tiers. "The Framework enables organizations -- regardless of size, degree of cybersecurity risk, or cybersecurity sophistication -- to apply the principles and best practices of risk management to improving the security and resilience of critical infrastructure."[9]

---

[8] http://www.whitehouse.gov/the-press-office/2013/02/12/executive-order-improving-critical-infrastructure-cybersecurity
[9] http://www.nist.gov/cyberframework/upload/cybersecurity-framework-021214.pdf

Chairwoman COMSTOCK. The Subcommittee on Research and Technology will come to order.

Without objection, the Chair is authorized to declare recesses of the Subcommittee at any time. We might be having some votes, I understand. I would just like to welcome everyone to today's hearing entitled ''The Expanding Cyber Threat.''

Without objection, the Chair authorizes the participation of Mr. Lipinski, Ms. Lofgren, Ms. Bonamici, Ms. Clark, and Mr. Beyer for today's hearing. I understand Mr. Lipinski will serve as the Ranking Minority Member today and give an opening statement.

In front of you are packets containing the written testimony, biographies, and truth-in-testimony disclosures for today's witnesses.

Now, I will recognize myself for five minutes for an opening statement.

Okay. I want to begin by thanking everyone for attending the first hearing of the Research and Technology Subcommittee in the 114th Congress. I look forward to working with the Members of the Subcommittee on the many issues that fall under the jurisdiction of this Subcommittee.

The need to secure our information technology systems is a pervasive concern. Today's hearing marks the first of what will be several hearings, I imagine, to examine the topic of cybersecurity. We know we heard the President speak about this and we have—and the Chairman has been a big advocate of increased activity and concerns on this front so I look forward to continuing to work on this issue.

The Subcommittee has jurisdiction over the National Science Foundation, the National Institute of Standards and Technology and the Department of Homeland Security's Science and Technology Directorate. These organizations play a role in supporting basic research and development, establishing standards and best practices, and working with industry on cybersecurity concerns. Advances in technology and the growing nature of every individual's online presence means cybersecurity needs to become an essential part of our everyday life.

Instances of harmful cyber attacks are in the news regularly and expose the very real threats growing in this area. Financial information, medical records, personal data maintained on computer systems by individuals and organizations all continue to be vulnerable. Cyber attacks on companies like Sony or Target, as well as the U.S. Central Command, will not go away and we have to constantly adapt and intercept and stop these threats and engage in finding the best practices so that we make sure these attacks don't happen and we understand where and how they are coming at us and how we can stay ever vigilant.

Utilizing targeted emails, spam, malware, bots and other tools, cyber criminals, ''hacktivists'' and nation states are every day attempting to access information technology systems all over the world and all over our country and in every area of our activities. The defense of these systems relies on professionals who can react to threats and proactively prepare those systems for attack.

Our discussion about cybersecurity should examine the research that supports understanding how to defend and support our systems, as well as how to better prepare our workforce by producing experts in these fields and learning of best practices in both the public and private sector. Well-trained professionals are essential to the implementation of the best techniques. Institutions of higher education are working to create and improve cyber education and training programs focused on ensuring there are enough trained professionals to meet the needs of this growing industry.

I look forward to hearing from our witnesses today as they provide an overview of the state of cybersecurity from the industry perspective and we learn how the federal government is playing a role in this important area.

[The prepared statement of Ms. Comstock follows:]

PREPARED STATEMENT OF SUBCOMMITTEE
CHAIRWOMAN BARBARA COMSTOCK

I want to begin by thanking everyone for attending the first hearing of the Research and Technology Subcommittee in the 114th Congress. I look forward to working with the Members of the Subcommittee on the many issues that fall under the jurisdiction of this Subcommittee.

The need to secure our information technology systems is a pervasive concern. Today's hearing marks the first of what will be several hearings to examine the topic of cybersecurity.

The Subcommittee has jurisdiction over the National Science Foundation, the National Institute of Standards and Technology and the Department of Homeland Security's Science and Technology Directorate. These organizations play a role in supporting basic research and development, establishing standards and best practices, and working with industry on cybersecurity concerns.

Advances in technology and the growing nature of every individual's online presence means cybersecurity needs to become an essential part of our vernacular.

Instances of harmful cyber-attacks are reported regularly and expose the very real threats growing in this area. Financial information, medical records, and personal data maintained on computer systems by individuals and organizations continue to be vulnerable. Cyber-attacks on companies like Sony or Target and the U.S. Central Command will not go away and we have to constantly adapt and intercept and stop these threats before they happen and understand where and how they are happening and stay ever vigilant.

Utilizing targeted emails, spam, malware, bots and other tools, cyber criminals, "hacktivists" and nation states are attempting to access information technology systems all the time. The defense of these systems relies on professionals who can react to threats and proactively prepare those systems for attack.

Our discussions about cybersecurity should examine the research that supports understanding how to defend and support our systems as well as how to better prepare our workforce by producing experts in these fields and learning of best practices in both the public and private sector. Well-trained professionals are essential to the implementation of security techniques. Institutions of higher education are working to create and improve cyber education and training programs focused on ensuring there are enough trained professionals to meet the needs of industry.

I look forward to hearing from our witnesses today as they provide an overview of the state of cybersecurity from the industry perspective and we learn how the federal government is playing a role in this important area.

Chairwoman COMSTOCK. Now, I would like to recognize Ranking Member Mr. Lipinski for his opening statement.

Mr. LIPINSKI. Thank you, Chairwoman Comstock, for holding this hearing on cybersecurity and I want to welcome you to the Science, Space, and Technology Committee. I am looking forward to working with you. I know that you worked for former member Frank Wolf and Frank Wolf was—I have a tremendous amount of respect for him and he was a big supporter of funding for research. He is a big supporter of research and technology, science, so I think hopefully we will have a lot of things that we can work together on on this Subcommittee, on the Committee.

I also want to thank our witnesses for being here today on this very important topic.

Cybersecurity remains a timely topic, the topic on which this Committee has an important role, and finally, is one for which we have much more agreement than disagreement across the aisle. So I am pleased that the Research and Technology Subcommittee is starting off the new Congress with this hearing.

Cyber crimes are ever increasing. The threats are not only growing in number but in level of sophistication. Some cases, such as the recent Sony hack and a 2013 Target breach, are very high profile and are covered extensively in the media. Many, many more receive less attention. Two weeks ago the New York Times reported that hacking has gone mainstream. A website has been created to connect hackers to potential clients. And as of early January, at least 500 hacking jobs have been laid out to bid and at least 50 hackers signed up to do the dirty work.

Cyber crime threatens our privacy, our pocketbooks, our safety, our economy, and our national security. Arriving at any precise value of losses to the American people and American economy is impossible, but the Center for Strategic and International Studies, in a study completed last June, reported that on average the United States loses .64 percent of its GDP to cybercrime. I know we will hear much more from our witnesses about the extent and the nature of the cyber threat.

Two years ago President Obama signed an Executive Order to begin the process of strengthening our networks and critical infrastructure against cyber attack by increasing information-sharing and establishing a framework for the development of standards and best practices, and this plays a key role in several of these efforts. You will hear about some of it today. But the President reminded us just two weeks ago that Congress must still act to pass comprehensive cybersecurity legislation. Fortunately, this is one area in which this Committee has responsibly legislated in the last few years.

At the very end of 2014, the Cybersecurity Enhancement Act that I joined Mr. McCaul in introducing for several Congresses in a row was finally signed into law. That law does a number of things: it strengthens coordination and strategic planning for federal cybersecurity R&D; it codifies the NIST-led voluntary framework in the President's Executive Order; it strengthens and streamlines NIST-led processes by which federal agencies track security risks to their own systems; it codifies NSF's long-standing CyberSecurity Scholarship for Service program to ensure more qualified cyber experts are employed by federal, state, and local governments; it codifies the cybersecurity education and awareness efforts led by NIST; and finally, it authorizes several more important actions and programs led by NIST.

I list all of these things in part so that all of the new members of the Science Committee understand just how essential NIST is to our government's cybersecurity efforts. It is one of the most important, least-known agencies in our government. I look forward to hearing about NIST's effort from Dr. Romine and how the new law will further strengthen NIST's leadership role in cybersecurity.

I also look forward to hearing from Dr. Kurose about the critical and potentially transformative cybersecurity research programs funded by the National Science Foundation.

And I look forward to hearing from the other three witnesses who can help educate us further about the importance of public-private partnerships and the areas where this Committee might look to address cybersecurity vulnerabilities during this Congress.

Thank you, Madam Chairwoman, and I yield back the balance of my time.

[The prepared statement of Mr. Lipinski follows:]

PREPARED STATEMENT OF SUBCOMMITTEE
MINORITY RANKING MEMBER DANIEL LIPINSKI

Thank you, Chairwoman Comstock for holding this hearing on cybersecurity, and welcome to the Science, Space, and Technology Committee. I look forward to working with you this Congress. I also want to thank our witnesses for being here today.

Cybersecurity remains a timely topic, it is a topic on which this Committee has an important role, and finally it is one for which we have much more agreement than disagreement across the aisle. So I am pleased that the Research and Technology Subcommittee is starting off the new Congress with this hearing.

Cybercrimes are ever-increasing. The threats are not only growing in number, but in the level of sophistication. Some cases, such as the recent Sony hack and the 2013 Target breach, are very high profile and are covered extensively in the media. Many, many more receive less attention. Two weeks ago, the New York Times reported that hacking has gone mainstream. A website has been created to connect hackers to potential clients, and as of early January, at least 500 hacking jobs had been laid out to bid and at least 50 hackers signed up to do the dirty work.

Cybercrime threatens our privacy, our pocketbooks, our safety, our economy, and our national security. Arriving at any precise value of losses to the American people and the American economy is impossible. But the Center for Strategic and International Studies, in a study completed last June, reported that, on average, the U.S. loses 0.64 percent of its GDP to cybercrime. I know we will hear more from our witnesses about the extent and nature of the cyber threat.

Two years ago, President Obama signed an Executive Order to begin the process of strengthening our networks and critical infrastructure against cyberattack by increasing information sharing and establishing a framework for the development of standards and best practices. NIST plays a key role in several of these efforts, and we will hear about some of it today. But the President reminded us just two weeks ago that Congress must still act to pass comprehensive cybersecurity legislation.

Fortunately, this is one area in which this Committee has responsibly legislated in the last few years. At the very end of 2014, the Cybersecurity Enhancement Act that I joined Mr. McCaul in introducing for several Congresses in a row was finally signed into law. That law does a number of things.

- It strengthens coordination and strategic planning for federal cybersecurity R&D;
- It codifies the NIST-led voluntary Framework in the President's Executive Order;
- It strengthens and streamlines the NIST-led processes by which federal agencies track security risks to their own systems;
- It codifies NSF's longstanding cybersecurity scholarship for service program to ensure more qualified cyber experts are employed by federal, state, and local governments;
- It codifies the cybersecurity education and awareness efforts led by NIST;
- And finally it authorizes several more important actions and programs led by NIST.

I list all of these things in part so that all of the new Members to the Science Committee understand just how central NIST is to our government's cybersecurity efforts. It is one of the most important leastknown agencies in our government. I look forward to hearing about NIST's efforts from Dr. Romine, and how the new law will further strengthen NIST's leadership role in cybersecurity. I also look forward to hearing from Dr. Kurose about the critical and potentially transformative cybersecurity research programs funded by the National Science Foundation. And I look forward to hearing from the other three witnesses who can help educate us further about the importance of public-private partnerships and the areas where this Committee might look to address cybersecurity vulnerabilities during this Congress.

Thank you, Madam Chairwoman and I yield back the balance of my time.

Chairwoman COMSTOCK. And now I recognize the Chairman of the full Committee, Mr. Smith.

Chairman SMITH. And thank you, Madam Chair.

Madam Chair, let me say I look forward to your Chairing this Subcommittee and also to the gentleman from Illinois, Mr. Lipinski, continuing to be the Ranking Member of this Subcommittee as well. He has been a great Ranking Member and I know that we both will all be able to work together for more bipartisan legislation that we enjoyed in the last Congress and that we can look forward to in this new Congress as well.

I also look forward to today's hearing on cyber threats, a topic that continues to grow in importance. With technological advances come new methods that foreign countries, cyber criminals and ''hacktivists'' use to attack and access our networks.

America is vulnerable and there is an increasing need for technically trained cybersecurity experts to identify and defend against cyber attacks. Protecting America's cyber systems is critical to our economic and national security.

As our reliance on information technology expands, so do our vulnerabilities. A number of federal agencies guard America's cybersecurity interests. Several are under the jurisdiction of the Science Committee. These include the National Science Foundation, the National Institute of Standards and Technology, the Department of Homeland Security's Science and Technology Directorate, and the Department of Energy. All of these support critical research and development to promote cybersecurity in hardware, software and our critical infrastructure.

At the beginning of the last Congress, the Science Committee considered two cybersecurity bills, the Cybersecurity Enhancement Act and a bill to reauthorize the Networking and Information Technology Research and Development program. Both bills passed the House last April. At the end of the last Congress, the House and Senate did come to an agreement on the Cybersecurity Enhancement Act, which was signed into law in December. The Science Committee will continue its efforts to support the research and development essential to fortifying our nation's cyber defenses.

From the theft of credit card information at retailers like Target and Home Depot, to successful attacks at Sony and on the U.S. Central Command, no further wakeup calls are necessary to understand our call to action. As America continues to become more advanced, we must better protect our information technology systems from attack. Any real solution should adapt to changing technology and tactics while also protecting private sector companies, public institutions and personal privacy.

Again, Madam Chair, I look forward to today's hearing and yield back.

[The prepared statement of Mr. Smith follows:]

PREPARED STATEMENT OF FULL COMMITTEE
CHAIRMAN LAMAR S. SMITH

Thank you Madam Chair, I look forward to today's hearing on cyber threats, a topic that continues to grow in importance.

In the 60 years since the last major patent reform, America has experienced tremendous technological advancements. Computers the size of a closet have evolved into wireless technology that fits in the palm of our hand.

With technological advances come new methods that foreign countries, cyber criminals and ''hacktivists'' can use to attack and access our networks.

America is vulnerable and there is an increasing need for technically-trained cybersecurity experts to identify and defend against cyber-attacks. Protecting America's cyber-systems is critical to our economic and national security. As our reliance on information technology expands, so do our vulnerabilities.

A number of federal agencies guard America's cybersecurity interests. Several are under the jurisdiction of the Science Committee. These include the National Science Foundation (NSF), the National Institute of Standards and Technology (NIST), the Department of Homeland Security's Science and Technology Directorate, and the Department of Energy.

All of these support critical research and development to promote cybersecurity in hardware, software and our critical infrastructure.

At the beginning of the last Congress, the Science Committee considered two cybersecurity bills, the Cybersecurity Enhancement Act and a bill to reauthorize the Networking and Information Technology Research and Development program. Both bills passed the House in April 2013.

At the end of the last Congress, the House and Senate came to agreement on the Cybersecurity Enhancement Act, which was signed into law in December. That law improves America's cybersecurity abilities. It strengthens strategic planning for cybersecurity research and development needs across the federal government. It supports NSF scholarships to improve the quality of the cybersecurity workforce. And it improves research, development and public outreach organized by NIST related to cybersecurity.

The Science Committee will continue its efforts to support the research and development essential to fortifying our nation's cyber defenses.

From the theft of credit card information at retailers like Target and Home Depot, to successful attacks at Sony and on the U.S. Central Command, no further wake-up calls are necessary to understand our call to action.

As America continues to become more advanced, we must better protect our information technology systems from attack. Any real solution should adapt to changing technology and tactics while also protecting private sector companies, public institutions and personal privacy.

I look forward to hearing from our witnesses today and yield back.

Chairwoman COMSTOCK. If there are Members who wish to submit additional opening statements, your statements will be added to the record at this point.

Chairwoman COMSTOCK. I would also like to welcome our colleague from Washington, Mr. Newhouse, and authorize his participation in today's hearing.

Okay. Now, at this time I would like to introduce our witnesses. Our first witness today is Ms. Cheri McGuire. Ms. McGuire is the Vice President of Global Government Affairs & Cybersecurity Policy at Symantec Corporation. Before joining Symantec, Ms. McGuire served as Director for Critical Infrastructure and Cybersecurity in Microsoft's Trustworthy Computing Group and as Acting Director at DHS's National Cybersecurity Division. Ms. McGuire received her bachelor's degree from the University of California Riverside and her MBA from the George Washington University.

Our second witness is Dr. James Kurose. Dr. Kurose is the National Science Foundation's Assistant Director for the Computer and Information Science and Engineering Directorate. He also serves as Co-Chair of the Networking and Information Technology

Research and Development Subcommittee at the National Science and Technology Council Committee on Technology.

Now, do you say all that when—in one introduction? That is good.

Prior to joining NSF, Dr. Kurose was a distinguished Professor in the School of Computer Science at the University of Massachusetts Amherst where he served as Chair of the Department of Computer Science. Dr. Kurose holds a bachelor's degree in physics from Wesleyan University and a Master of Science and Ph.D. in computer science from Columbia University.

Our third witness today is Dr. Charles Romine, Director of the National Institute of Standards and Technology Information Technology Laboratory, or ITL. Before working at NIST he served as Senior Policy Analyst at the White House Office of Science and Technology Policy and as a Program Manager at the Department Of Energy's Advanced Scientific Computing Research Office. Dr. Romine received his bachelor's degree in mathematics and his Ph.D. in applied mathematics from the University of Virginia. Yea.

Our fourth witness is Dr. Eric Fischer, who serves as a Senior Specialist in the Science and Technology for the Congressional Research Service. Prior to working for CRS, Dr. Fischer worked as a faculty member at the University of Washington in Seattle and as a Congressional Science and Technology Policy Fellow for the American Association for the Advancement of Science. Dr. Fischer received his bachelor's degree in biology from Yale and his Ph.D. in zoology from the University of California Berkeley.

Our final witness is Mr. Dean Garfield, President and CEO of the Information Technology Industry Council, or ITI. Before joining ITI, Mr. Garfield served as Executive Vice President and Chief Strategic Officer for the Motion Picture Association of America and as the Vice President of Legal Affairs at the Recording Industry Association of America. Mr. Garfield received a joint degree from New York University School of Law and the Woodrow Wilson School of Public Administration and International Affairs at Princeton University.

As our witnesses should know, spoken testimony is limited to five minutes each, after which the Members of the Committee will have five minutes each to ask questions.

I now recognize Ms. McGuire for five minutes to present her testimony.

TESTIMONY OF MS. CHERI MCGUIRE, VICE PRESIDENT, GLOBAL GOVERNMENT AFFAIRS & CYBERSECURITY POLICY, SYMANTEC CORPORATION

Ms. McGuire. Chairwoman Comstock, Chairman Smith, Ranking Member Lipinski, and other Members of the Subcommittee, thank you for the opportunity to testify today on behalf of Symantec Corporation.

My name is Cheri McGuire and I am the Vice President for Global Government Affairs and Cybersecurity Policy. At Symantec we are the largest security software company in the world and our global intelligence network is made up of millions of sensors that give us a unique view into the entire internet threat landscape.

As I am sure you have read, most of the recent headlines about cyber attacks have focused on data breaches and the theft of personally identifiable information, including identities and credit card numbers. According to Symantec's most recent internet security threat report, over 550 million identities were exposed in 2013 alone. Yet while the focus on these breaches is certainly warranted, it is important not to lose sight of other equally concerning types of cyber activity. Attackers run the gamut and include highly organized criminal enterprises, individual cyber criminals, so-called hacktivists, and state-sponsored groups. Common attack types range from distributed denial of service, or DDoS, to highly targeted attacks, to widely distributed financial fraud scams. A DDoS attack is an attempt to overwhelm a system with data, while targeted attacks tried to trick someone into opening an infected file or navigating to a bad website.

Of course, scams and blackmail schemes seeking money continue. Some will fill a victim's screen with aggressive pop-up windows that claim falsely that the system is infected. Others lock the victim's computer and display a screen that purports to be from law enforcement and demands payment of a fine for having illegal content on the computer. The most recent scheme has gone from trickery to straight up blackmail. Criminals now will encrypt or scramble all the data on your device and tell you to pay a ransom or they will erase all of it.

Critical infrastructure such as the power grid, water system, and mass transit are also at risk. In June 2014 Symantec released a report about a new threat that we named Dragonfly. This was a campaign against a range of targets mainly in the energy sector, but it was not the first to target energy. As we saw in 2012, cyber attackers mounted a campaign against the Saudi Arabian National Oil Company that destroyed 30,000 computers and made them display the image of a burning American flag. Other sectors have seen attacks, too, and the German Government recently disclosed that a cyber attack on a steel plant resulted in massive physical damage.

All of the attacks that I have outlined started with a common factor, a compromised computer. We frequently hear about advanced persistent threats, or APTs, but the discussion of cyber attacks too often ignores the psychology of the exploit. Most rely on social engineering, in the simplest terms, trying to trick people into doing something that they would never do if fully aware of their actions.

Attack methods vary. Those spear fishing or customized targeted emails containing malware are the most common, and while good security will stop most of these attacks, which often seek to exploit older known vulnerabilities, many organizations and individuals do not have up-to-date security or properly patched operating systems. Social media is also an increasingly valuable tool for cyber criminals both to gather information and to spread malicious links.

To combat cyber threats, Symantec partners with government and industry here and abroad. Working extensively with the FBI and international law enforcement, we have helped take down and dismantle some of the world's largest botnets, which has also led to charges against the criminal operators.

In addition, together with Palo Alto Networks, McAfee, and Fortinet, we recently cofounded the Cyber Threat Alliance, a group of cybersecurity providers who share advanced cyber threat information. While we are competitors, we have found that there is great benefit to sharing information that will protect all of our customers and help fight cyber criminals. This model has worked well in other sectors such as banking and energy. And further, and even as important, the alliance has strict guidelines that protect our customer privacy and their proprietary information, and this of course must be included in any information-sharing regime.

So what can we do? Good protection starts with a plan and strong security should include intrusion protection, reputation-based security, behavioral-based blocking, data encryption, backups, and data loss prevention tools. And while the criminals' tactics are constantly evolving, basic cyber hygiene is still the simplest and most cost-effective first step.

Last week, the Online Trust Alliance found that 90 percent of last year's breaches could have been prevented if businesses implemented basic cyber best practices. At Symantec we are committed to improving online security across the globe and we will continue to work collaboratively with our partners on ways to do so.

Thank you again for the opportunity to testify today and I look forward to your questions.

[The prepared statement of Ms. McGuire follows:]

Prepared Testimony and
Statement for the Record of

Cheri F. McGuire
Vice President, Global Government Affairs & Cybersecurity Policy
Symantec Corporation

Hearing on

"The Expanding Cyber Threat"

Before the

House Committee on Science, Space, and Technology
Subcommittee on Research and Technology

January 27, 2015

2318 Rayburn House Office Building

Distinguished members of the Subcommittee, thank you for the opportunity to testify today on behalf of Symantec Corporation.

My name is Cheri McGuire and I am the Vice President for Global Government Affairs and Cybersecurity Policy at Symantec. I am responsible for Symantec's global public policy agenda and government engagement strategy, which includes cybersecurity, data integrity, critical infrastructure protection (CIP), and privacy. I lead a team of professionals spanning the U.S., Canada, Europe, and Asia, and represent the company in key policy organizations. In this capacity, I work extensively with industry and government organizations, and currently serve on the World Economic Forum Global Agenda Council on Cybersecurity as well as on the boards of the Information Technology Industry Council, the US Information Technology Office (USITO) in China, and the National Cyber Security Alliance. From 2010 to 2012 I was Chair of the Information Technology Sector Coordinating Council (IT SCC) – one of 16 critical sectors identified by the President and the US Department of Homeland Security (DHS) to partner with the government on CIP and cybersecurity. I am also a past board member of the IT Information Sharing and Analysis Center (IT-ISAC). Previously, I served in various positions at DHS, including as head of the National Cyber Security Division and US Computer Emergency Readiness Team (US-CERT).

Symantec protects much of the world's information, and is a global leader in security, backup and availability solutions. We are the largest security software company in the world, with over 32 years of experience developing Internet security technology and helping consumers, businesses and governments secure and manage their information and identities. Our products and services protect people's information and their privacy across platforms – from the smallest mobile device, to the enterprise data center, to cloud-based systems. We have established some of the most comprehensive sources of Internet threat data in the world through our Global Intelligence Network, which is comprised of millions of attack sensors recording thousands of events per second, and we maintain 10 Security Response Centers around the globe. In addition, we process billions of e-mail messages and web requests across our 14 global data centers. All of these resources allow us to capture worldwide security data that give our analysts a unique view of the entire Internet threat landscape.

The cyber headlines of the past year have focused largely on massive data breaches, but that is just one corner of the cyber threat landscape. In my testimony today, I will discuss:

- Some common types of attacks;
- Methods attackers use to compromise systems;
- Partnering to fight cybercrime; and
- How individuals and organizations can protect themselves.

The Current Cyber Threat Landscape

Most of the recent headlines about cyber attacks have focused on data breaches across the spectrum of industries. Sadly, breaches have become an all too common occurrence, impacting not only those breached but also creating geo-political challenges for governments around the world. The organizations that suffered significant breaches over the past year include a "who's who" of the business world: Target, Michael's, Home Depot, The New York Times, and Sony are just a sampling of recent victims.

The theft of personally identifiable information (PII) in this timeframe was unprecedented. According to our most recent Internet Security Threat Report (ISTR), over 550 million identities were exposed in 2013, and eight different breaches exposed 10 million identities or more. We expect that our final statistics from 2014 will be similarly alarming. Interestingly, the Online Trust Alliance just released a report that found that 90% of last year's breaches could have been prevented if businesses relooked at their cyber risk strategies and implemented basic cyber best practices.[1]

While the focus on these public breaches and the identities put at risk is certainly warranted, it is important not to lose sight of the other types of cyber activity that are equally concerning and that can also have dangerous and broad consequences. There are a wide range of tools available to the cyber attacker, and the attacks we see today range from basic confidence schemes to massive denial of service attacks to sophisticated (and potentially destructive) intrusions into critical infrastructure systems. The economic impact can be immediate with the theft of money, or more long term and structural, such as through the theft of intellectual property. It can ruin a company or individual's reputation or finances, and it can impact citizens' trust in their government.

Attackers run the gamut and include highly organized criminal enterprises, individual cybercriminals, so-called "hacktivists," and state-sponsored groups. The motivations vary – the criminals generally are looking for some type of financial gain, the hacktivists are seeking to promote or advance some cause, and the state actors can be engaged in espionage (whether traditional spycraft or economic espionage) or infiltrating critical infrastructure systems. These lines, however, are not set in stone, as criminals and even state actors might pose as hacktivists, and criminals sometimes will offer their skills to the highest bidder. Attribution has always been difficult in the cyber landscape, and is further complicated by the ability of cyber actors to mask their motives and objectives through misdirection and obfuscation.

Common Types of Attacks

Distributed Denial of Service ("DDoS")

Distributed denial-of-service (DDoS) attacks attempt to deny service to legitimate users by overwhelming the target with activity. The most common method is to flood a server with network traffic from multiple sources (hence "distributed"). These attacks are often conducted through "botnets" – armies of compromised computers that are made up of victim machines that stretch across the globe and are controlled by "bot herders" or "bot masters."[2] One recent study found that over 60% of traffic on the internet today is from bots.[3]

DDoS attacks have grown larger year over year and in 2014 some attacks reached 400 Gigabits per second, a previously unimaginable volume of data. This is roughly equivalent to blasting a network every second with the data stored on more than 10 DVDs. In the past few years we have seen attacks go from the equivalent of a garden hose to a fire hose to the outflow pipes of the Hoover dam. Even the most prepared networks can buckle under that volume of data the first time it is directed at them, which is why even some of the country's biggest financial institutions initially suffered outages from recent DDoS attacks. In addition to increasing in volume, the attacks are getting more sophisticated and varying the methods used, which makes them harder to mitigate. In particular, in 2014 attackers used new techniques to amplify the strength of an attack which made it easier for even the "average" attack to reach levels of volume that were unthinkable just years before.[4]

---

[1] https://www.otalliance.org/news-events/press-releases/ota-determines-over-90-data-breaches-2014-could-have-been-prevented

[2] "Bots and Botnets – A Growing Threat," *Symantec,* http://us.norton.com/botnet/

[3] Igal Zeifman, "Report: Bot Traffic is up to 61.5% of all Website Traffic," *Incapsula,* December 9, 2013, http://incapsula.com/blog/bot-traffic-report-2013.html.

[4] Symantec, *"Security Response: The Continued Rise of DDoS Attacks,"* October 21, 2014, Pg. 25.

According to a survey by Neustar, 60% of companies were impacted by a DDoS attack in 2013 and 87 percent were hit more than once.[5] The most affected sectors were the gaming, media, and software industries. The purpose of most attacks is to disrupt, not to destroy. Cybercriminals can rent DDoS attack services on the black market for as little as $5, allowing them to conduct a short, minutes-long DDoS attack against any chosen target (fig. 1).[6] If successful, even such a short attack is enough to garner attention – or to distract an organization's security team, as another recent use of DDoS attacks has been to provide cover for other, more sophisticated attacks. Organized crime groups have been known to launch DDoS attacks against banks to divert the attention and resources of the bank's security team while the main attack is launched, which can include draining customer accounts or stealing credit card information.

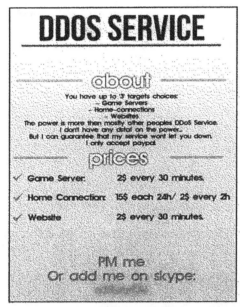

Fig. 1. Example of a DDoS service for hire – this one is directed at online gamers.

Targeted Attacks

Targeted attacks are another tool in the cybercriminal's tool box, and the attached graphic illustrates some common attack methods as well as the economics of cybercrime (see *Path of A Cybercriminal*, attached on page 12). Some attacks are directed at a company's servers and systems, where attackers search for unpatched vulnerabilities on websites or undefended connections to the internet. But most rely on social engineering – in the simplest of terms, trying to trick people into doing something that they would never do if fully aware of their actions. They can be targeted at almost any level, even at an entire sector of the economy or a group of similar organizations or companies. They also can target a particular company or a unit within the company (*e.g.*, research and development or finance) or even a specific person.

Most of the data breaches and other attacks that have been in the news were the result of a targeted attack, but the goal of the attacker can vary greatly. One constant is that after attackers select a target

---

[5] Neustar, *"2014, The Danger Deepens: Neustar Annual DDoS Attacks and Impact Report,"* June 2014, Pg. 3.
[6] Symantec, *"Security Response: The Continued Rise of DDoS Attacks,"* October 21, 2014, Pg. 12.

they will set out to gain access to the systems they want to compromise and once inside there are few limits on what they can do if the system is not well-protected. The malware used today is largely commoditized, and while we still see some that is custom-crafted, most of the attacks rely on attack kits that are sold on the cyber black market. But even these commodity attack kits are highly sophisticated and are designed to avoid detection – some even come with guarantees from the criminal seller that they will not be stopped by common security measures. This makes it all the more important – but also more challenging – to stay ahead of them.

Scams, Blackmail, and other Cyber Theft

Like most crime, cyber attacks are often financially motivated, and some of the most common (and most successful) involve getting victims to pay out money, whether through trickery or direct threats. One early and widely successful attack of this type was known as "scareware" (fig. 2). Scareware is a form of malware that will open a window on your device that claims your system is infected, and offer to "clean" it for a fee. Some forms of scareware open pop-ups claiming to be from major security companies (including Symantec), and if a user clicks in the window they are taken to a fake website that can look very much like that of the real company. Of course, in most cases the only infection on your computer is the scareware itself. Victims are lucky if they only lose the $20 or $30 "cost" for the fake software, but most are out much more as they typically provide credit card information to pay the scammer in the mistaken belief they are purchasing legitimate security software. Not only did they authorize a payment to the scammer, but they also provided financial information that could then be sold on the criminal underground. And by allowing the scammer to install the supposed cleaning software on their device, they give the criminal the ability to install additional malware and potentially steal more financial information or turn their system into a zombie soldier in a botnet.

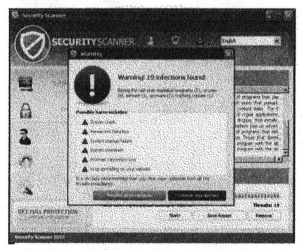

Fig. 2. An example of Scareware. The pop-ups proclaim that the victim's computer is infected, and often cannot be closed.

First widely seen in 2007, scareware began to diminish in 2011 after users became alerted to the scams and they became much less effective. Nevertheless, criminals have made millions from this type of scam.

Once scareware began to be less effective, criminals turned to "ransomware," and it has grown significantly since 2012. Ransomware is another type of deception where the malware locks the victim's device and displays a screen that purports to be from a law enforcement entity local to the user. The lock screen states that there is illegal content on the computer – everything from pirated movies to child pornography – and instructs the victim to pay a "fine" for their "crime" (fig. 3). The criminals claim that the victim's device will be unlocked once the "fine" is paid, but in reality the device frequently remains locked. Should your device become infected, it is important to disconnect it quickly from the Internet and any other computers or devices. This will help prevent the theft of additional personal information from your computer as well as keep the infection from spreading further and stop your computer from being used as part of a botnet. Both of these types of attacks can be removed from your computer and we offer instructions and free tools on our Norton.com website to assist victims in doing so. Unfortunately, some of the more sophisticated variants can require some expertise to remediate.

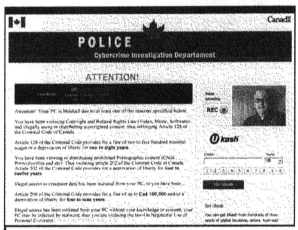

Fig. 3. This ransomware targeted victims in Canada; victims in other countries would see logos of law enforcement local to them. It used built-in webcams to take a victim's picture to further frighten them.

Unfortunately, criminals have moved beyond even ransomware and are now using a more insidious and harmful form of malware known as "ransomcrypt." While scareware and ransomware are more classic confidence schemes, ransomcrypt is straight-up blackmail: pay a ransom or your computer will be erased (fig. 4). And unlike scareware and ransomware, there is often no easy way to get rid of it – the criminals use high-grade encryption technology to scramble the victim's computer, and only they have the key to unlock it. Unless the system is backed up, the victim faces the difficult choice of paying the criminals or losing all the data, and there have been reports of even police departments paying to regain control of their systems.[7]

---

[7] John E. Dunn, "US police department pays $750 Cryptolocker Trojan ransom demand," *tech world*, November 19, 2013, http://www.techworld.com/news/security/us-police-department-pays-750-cryptolocker-trojan-ransom-demand-3489937/

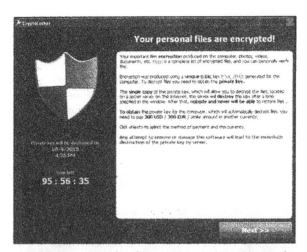

Fig. 4. This is a screenshot of Cryptolocker, a sophisticated piece of ransomcrypt that was disrupted this summer by an international takedown effort, in which Symantec participated.

This is not meant to suggest that the criminals are unstoppable; in fact, in June 2014 we were part of a team that helped take down Cryptolocker. Symantec assisted the FBI and several other international law enforcement agencies to mount a major operation during which authorities seized a large portion of the infrastructure that had been used by the cybercriminals. As a result of Symantec's research into the threat, we were able to provide technical insights into their operation and impact. Since June, the Cryptolocker infection rate has dropped to near zero. But other forms are still out there, and the fight goes on.

<u>Threats to Critical Infrastructure</u>

Critical infrastructure such as the power grid, water system, and mass transit are also at risk. As more of these devices become connected and are controlled remotely, attackers have more opportunities to try to exploit them. In June 2014, we notified and provided detailed Indicators of Compromise (IoC) to more than 40 national computer security incident response teams around the world about a new threat we named *DragonFly*.[8] This was an ongoing cyber espionage campaign against a range of targets, mainly in the energy sector, which gave attackers control over computers that they could have used to damage or destroy critical machinery and disrupt energy supplies in affected countries. Among the targets of *Dragonfly* were energy grid operators, electricity generation firms, petroleum pipeline operators, and industrial equipment providers – the majority of which were located in the U.S., Spain, France, Italy, Germany, Turkey, and Poland. Quick and detailed notification was critical in mitigating the threat.

This was not the first campaign targeted at the energy sector. In 2012, cyber attackers mounted a campaign against Saudi Arabia's national oil firm Saudi Aramco, which destroyed approximately 30,000 computers and took its network off line for days. The infected computers were rendered unusable and displayed the image of a burning American flag. Though operations were not impacted, there was speculation in the press that oil production was the ultimate target. Shortly after the Saudi Aramco attack, a Qatari producer of liquefied natural gas, RasGas, suffered a similar attack which damaged its networks

---

[8] Symantec, *"Security Response: Dragonfly: Western Energy Companies under Sabotage,"* June 30, 2014. http://www.symantec.com/connect/blogs/dragonfly-western-energy-companies-under-sabotage-threat

and took down its website. Other sectors have seen attacks too. In the manufacturing sector, the German Government recently disclosed that a cyber attack on a steel plant resulted in the failure of multiple components and, according to one report, "massive physical damage."[9]

In the U.S. we have yet to see major destructive attacks on critical infrastructure. However, there have been widespread reports that foreign actors have sought to gain a foothold on the networks of U.S. critical infrastructure providers.[10] And we have seen the actual compromise of one water treatment facility in South Houston, Texas (fig. 5), though the attacker did not alter any controls or settings and claimed to be trying to bring attention to the vulnerabilities that exist in critical infrastructure. This particular facility was not following security best practices and was still using default passwords that were widely known. There are undoubtedly many other critical systems that are similarly exposed.

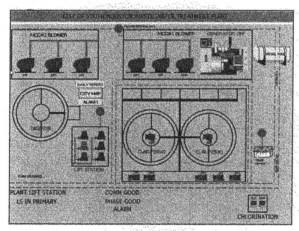

Fig. 5. Screenshot a hacker posted of the graphical user interface of the South Houston Waste Water Treatment Plant. He accessed this through use of an unchanged default user name and password.

Methods Attackers Use to Compromise Systems - Inside the Attacker's Tool Kit

All of the attacks outlined above started with a common factor – a compromised device. From this one computer, attackers often are able to move within a system until they achieve their ultimate goal. But the threshold question is how do they get that foothold – how do they make that initial compromise that allows them to infiltrate a system?

We frequently hear about the sophistication of various attackers and about "Advance Persistent Threats" or "APTs," but the discussion of cyber attacks – and of cyber defense – often ignores the psychology of the exploit. Most attacks rely on social engineering – in the simplest of terms, trying to trick people into doing something that they would never do if fully cognizant of their actions. For this reason, we often say that the most successful attacks are as much psychology as they are technology.

---

[9] SANS Industrial Control Systems (ICS), *"German Steel Mill Cyber Attack,"* December 30, 2014, Pg.1.
[10] Pierluigi Paganini, "The US energy industry is constantly under cyber attacks," *Security* Affairs, November 14, 2014 http://securityaffairs.co/wordpress/30328/cyber-crime/cyber-attacks-energy-industry.html

Spear phishing, or customized, targeted emails containing malware, is the most common form of attack. Attackers harvest publicly available information and use it to craft an email designed to dupe a specific victim or group of victims. The goal is to get victims to open a document or click on a link to a website that will then try to infect their computers. While good security will stop most of these attacks – which often seek to exploit older, known vulnerabilities – many organizations and individuals do not have up-to-date security or properly patched operating systems. And many of these attacks are extremely well-crafted; in the case of one major attack, the spear phishing email was so convincing that even though the victim's system automatically routed it to junk mail, he retrieved it and opened it – and exposed his company to a major breach.

Social media is an increasingly valuable tool for cyber criminals in two different ways. First, it is particularly effective in direct attacks, as people tend to trust links and postings that appear to come from a friend's social media feed and rarely stop to wonder if that feed may have been compromised or spoofed. Thus, attackers target social media accounts and then use them to "like" or otherwise promote a posting that contains a malicious link. But social media is also widely used to conduct reconnaissance for spear phishing or other highly targeted attacks as it often provides just the kind of personal details that a skilled attacker can use to get a victim to let his or her guard down. The old cliché is true when it comes to cyber attacks: we have to be right 100% of the time while the attacker only has to get it right once.

Beginning in 2012, we saw the rapid growth of a new type of targeted web-based attack, known as a "watering hole" attack. Like the lion in the wild who stalks a watering hole for unsuspecting prey, cybercriminals have become adept at lying in wait on legitimate websites and using them to try to infect visitors' computers. They do so by compromising legitimate websites that their victims are likely to visit and modifying them so that they will surreptitiously try to deliver malware to every visitor. For example, one attacker targeted mobile application developers by compromising a site that was popular with them. In another case, we saw employees from 500 different companies in the same industry visit one compromised site in just 24 hours, each running the risk of infection.[11] Cybercriminals gained control of these websites through many of the same tactics described above – spear phishing and other social engineering attacks on the site managers, developers, or owners. Many of these websites were compromised through known attack vectors, meaning that good security practices could have prevented them from being compromised.

Attackers will also periodically remove malware from an infected site to avoid regular security scans that might otherwise detect the compromise. At Symantec, we constantly scan websites for vulnerabilities and our Norton Safe Web will alert customers if they are trying to connect to a site that has vulnerabilities or might try to infect their computer with malware.

Partnering to Fight Cybercrime

To assist in combating cyber threats, Symantec participates in various industry organizations and public-private partnerships with all levels of governments in the U.S. and abroad.

We share high-level cybercrime and cyber threat trends and information on a voluntary basis through a number of different fora to help protect our customers and their networks. Effective sharing of actionable information among the public and private sectors on cyber threats, vulnerabilities, and incidents is an essential component of improving cybersecurity and combatting cybercrime. In 2014, together with Palo Alto Networks, Fortinet, and McAfee we co-founded the Cyber Threat Alliance (CTA), a group of

---

[11] Symantec, *"Internet Security Threat Report, Volume XVIII,"* April 16, 2013, Pg. 21.

cybersecurity providers, to share threat information to improve defenses against advanced cyber adversaries. The CTA adheres to strict guidelines that protect privacy and anonymize data, while at the same time pooling a broad array of resources to fight cybercriminals.

Symantec also has a formal partnership program whereby we work with government entities around the globe to help raise awareness, mitigate threats, share cyber threat information, assist in policy development and help with training and awareness. Partnership agreements include the EUROPOL's European Cybercrime Centre (EC3), the Korean National Police Agency, AMERIPOL and the Organization of American States (OAS), among others.

Symantec also partners with a number of non-profit organizations, including the Society for the Policing of Cyberspace (POLCYB), the National Cyber-Forensics and Training Alliance (NCFTA) and InfraGard. All three organizations are excellent examples of how private industry and law enforcement can yield real world success in the areas of training, criminal investigations and threat information sharing. Through POLCYB, Symantec provides training to law enforcement around the globe. Our partnership with the NCFTA includes more than 80 other industry partners — from financial services and telecommunications to manufacturing and others — working with federal and international partners to provide real-time cyber threat intelligence to an actionable level for law enforcement to neutralize those threats.

Law enforcement and the private sector – working together – have made significant progress in recent years. Not too long ago, numerous technological, cultural and organizational barriers prevented federal agencies from coordinating with each other or with industry on the investigation and prosecution of international cybercriminals. Those barriers have largely come down, and today we see that kind of cross-agency and public-private coordination on a regular basis.

Symantec's operation to bring down the ZeroAccess botnet, one of the largest botnets in history, estimated at 1.9 million infected devices, is a good example of how effective coordination between industry and law enforcement can yield results. A key feature of the ZeroAccess botnet was that it communicates widely across all infected computers rather than from a few command and control servers out to all those infected. This "peer to peer" architecture gives the botnet a high degree of availability and redundancy since it is not possible simply to disable a few servers and bring down the botnet. Early in 2013, Symantec's engineers identified a weakness that offered a difficult, but not impossible, way to shut down the botnet. Once we began to sinkhole ZeroAccess, over half a million bots were quickly detached, and later that year Microsoft filed a civil suit against the operators of the ZeroAccess botnet. These actions appear to have put an end to the botnet and the bot masters have halted their activity. They even included the words "White Flag" in the code of one of the last updates sent to infected computers.

Another significant win came in June of last year, when the FBI and a number of international law enforcement agencies mounted a major operation against financial fraud botnet Gameover Zeus and ransomware network Cryptolocker. We worked with the FBI and a broad industry coalition during this operation, and authorities seized a large proportion of the infrastructure used by the cybercriminals behind both threats. Gameover Zeus was the largest financial fraud botnet in operation last year and is often described as one of the most technically sophisticated variants of the ubiquitous Zeus malware.

A final example is the operation that helped to bring down the Bamital botnet, a major takedown that occurred in early 2013. This effort was the culmination of a multi-year investigation conducted by a public-private partnership including Symantec, Microsoft, and law enforcement. The Bamital botnet had taken over millions of computers for criminal activities such as identity theft and advertising-related fraud, and threatened the $12.7 billion online advertising industry. This successful takedown demonstrates what can be done when private industry and law enforcement join forces to go after cybercriminal networks.

It is also important to remember the toll that cybercrime takes on its victims. Part of our effort to stop cybercrime *writ large* is to focus on individual victims. In April of last year, we partnered with the National White Collar Crime Center (NWC3) to develop an online assistance program that helps cybercrime victims better understand the investigation process and help prevent future attacks. We also make tools available to the public to assist them if their computers are part of a botnet. In addition to our Norton Security software, we do offer some free tools online that allow victims of ransomware and botnets to remove this malware from their systems (http://www.symantec.com/security_response/removaltools.jsp).

How Individuals and Organizations Can Protect Themselves

The starting point for any organization is a plan that includes both proactive security measures and reactive steps to take in the event of an attack. Strong security is layered security, and must go beyond the basics such as good computer hygiene and antivirus software. It includes comprehensive protection that includes intrusion protection, reputation-based security, behavioral-based blocking, data encryption, and data loss prevention tools. Organizations should also back up their systems regularly so that they are protected from an attack that could destroy their data. There is no such thing as 100% security, but a layered defense approach to security can significantly reduce risk and a well-thought out and regularly exercised plan can mitigate any damage that might occur.

In addition, the NIST Cyber Security Framework, developed by industry and government in 2014 and in which Symantec was an active contributor, provides a solid structure for risk management. It lays out five core cybersecurity functions (Identify, Protect, Detect, Respond and Recover) that all organizations can use to plan for managing cyber events, as well as useful references to international standards.

Good security still starts with the basics. Though criminals' tactics are constantly evolving, basic cyber hygiene is still the simplest and most cost-effective first step. Strong passwords remain the foundation of good security – on home and work devices, email, social media accounts, or whatever you use to communicate or any sites or device you log into. And these passwords must be different, because using a single password means that a breach of one account exposes all of your accounts. Using a second authentication factor (whether a smart card, biometrics, or a token with a changing numeric password) significantly increases the security of a login.

Patch management of operating systems and other software applications is also critical. Individuals and organizations should not delay installing patches, because the same patch that closes a vulnerability on one computer can be a roadmap for a criminal to exploit that vulnerability and compromise any unpatched computers. The reality is that a large percentage of computers around the world do not get patched regularly, and cyber criminals count on this. While so-called "zero days" – previously unknown critical vulnerabilities for which there is not yet a patch – get the most press, it is older, un-patched vulnerabilities that cause most systems to get compromised.

But poor or insufficiently deployed security can also lead to a breach, and a modern security suite that is being fully utilized is also essential. While most people still commonly refer to security software as "anti-virus," good security needs to be much more than that. In the past, the same piece of malware would be delivered to thousands or even millions of computers. Today, cybercriminals can take the same malware and create unlimited unique variants that can slip past basic anti-virus software. If all your security software does is check for signatures (or digital fingerprints) of known malware, you are by definition not protected against even moderately sophisticated attacks.

Modern security software does much more than look for known malware; it monitors your computer, watching for unusual internet traffic, activity, or system processes that could be indicative of malicious activity. At Symantec we also use what we call Insight and SONAR, which are reputation-based and heuristic security technologies. Insight is a reputation-based technology that uses our Global Intelligence Network to put files in context, using their age, frequency, location and more to expose emerging threats that might otherwise be missed. If a computer is trying to execute a file that we have never seen anywhere in the world and that comes from an unknown source, there is a high probability that it is malicious – and Insight will block it.

Conclusion

Citizens are increasingly aware of the cyber risk and the need to take precautions to secure their data and protect their privacy. It is important that Americans know of the risk but also understand that there are things they can do to protect themselves. Every time someone patches their computer, changes a password, or utilizes a modern security suite, he or she is making it more difficult for cybercriminals to operate. Like any other crime, cybercrime will never be completely eliminated, but it can be fought. For example, the criminals did not stop using the scareware described above because they wanted to – they quit when it stopped working, and it stopped working when the targets no longer allowed themselves to be victimized.

At all levels, both government and industry recognize the imperative for cooperation to fight cybercrime. No single company or government can "go it alone" in the current threat landscape. The threats are too complex and the stakes are too high. Ultimately, stopping cyber attacks and the criminal networks behind them requires strong technical capabilities, effective countermeasures, industry collaboration and law enforcement cooperation to be successful. At Symantec, we are committed to improving online security across the globe, and will continue to work collaboratively with international industry and government partners on ways to do so. Thank you again for the opportunity to testify, and I will be happy to answer any questions you may have.

ATTACHMENT

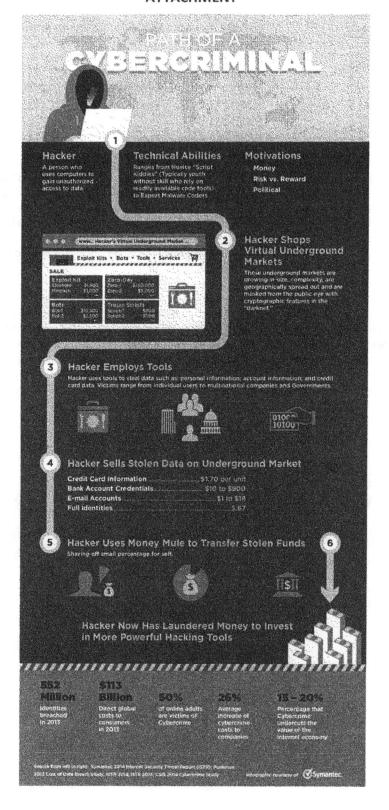

Cheri F. McGuire
Vice President, Global Government Affairs & Cybersecurity Policy
Symantec Corporation

Ms. Cheri McGuire serves as Vice President for Global Government Affairs and Cybersecurity Policy at Symantec. With more than twenty years of government and industry experience, Ms. McGuire is responsible for Symantec's global public policy agenda and government engagement strategy that includes cybersecurity, data integrity, critical infrastructure protection (CIP), and privacy. She leads a team of professionals spanning the United States, Canada, Europe and Asia, and represents the company in key public policy initiatives.

Ms. McGuire works extensively with industry and government organizations. She currently serves on the World Economic Forum Global Agenda Council on Cybersecurity, and on the boards of the Information Technology Industry Council, the US Information Technology Office (USITO) in China, and the National Cyber Security Alliance. From 2010 to 2012, she served as Chair of the US IT Sector Coordinating Council – one of 16 critical sectors identified by the President and the US Department of Homeland Security (DHS) to partner with the government on CIP and cybersecurity. She also is a past board member of the IT Information Sharing and Analysis Center, and a former member of the Industry Executive Subcommittee of the President's National Security Telecommunications Advisory Committee.

Ms. McGuire is a frequent presenter on technology policy issues, including testifying four times before the US Congress on cybersecurity, privacy and cybercrime. In addition, she was a speaker at the 2013 Seoul International Cyberspace Conference, the 2012 Budapest Conference on Cyberspace, the United Nations Economic and Social Council plenary session on cybersecurity and development in 2011, and the International Telecommunication Union (ITU) Plenipotentiary special session on cybersecurity in 2010.

Prior to joining Symantec in 2010, Ms. McGuire served as Director for Critical Infrastructure and Cybersecurity in Microsoft's Trustworthy Computing Group. From 2005 to 2008, she served in numerous positions at DHS, including as Acting Director and Deputy Director of the National Cyber Security Division and US-CERT. In this capacity, she provided leadership for DHS on the Comprehensive National Cybersecurity Initiative (CNCI) released by the President in January 2008, led the implementation of the 2008 National Cyber Exercise – Cyber Storm II, and was Head of US Delegation for bilateral cybersecurity talks with Japan in 2007.

Prior to DHS, she served as a program manager for Booz Allen Hamilton for nearly five years specializing in government telecom and computer security agencies, as a manager for a telecom engineering firm that was acquired by Exelon Infrastructure Services, and as a Congressional staffer for seven years. Ms. McGuire holds an MBA from The George Washington University and a BA from the University of California, Riverside.

Chairwoman COMSTOCK. I now recognize Dr. Kurose.

**TESTIMONY OF DR. JAMES KUROSE,
ASSISTANT DIRECTOR,
COMPUTER AND INFORMATION SCIENCE AND
ENGINEERING (CISE) DIRECTORATE,
NATIONAL SCIENCE FOUNDATION.**

Dr. KUROSE. Thank you. Good afternoon, Chairwoman Comstock, Chairman Smith, and Representative Lipinski, and Members of the Subcommittee. I am Jim Kurose, National Science Foundation Assistant Director for Computer and Information Science and Engineering. As you know, NSF advances and supports fundamental research in all disciplines, advances the progress of science and engineering, and educates the next generation of innovative leaders. I welcome this opportunity to provide an overview of NSF-funded cybersecurity research and its impact on the nation.

Long-term unclassified research is critical to achieving a secure and trustworthy cyberspace. In 2011 NSF contributed to the Administration's Strategic Plan for Federal Cybersecurity Research and Development. It specifies a coordinated research agenda for agency investments that change the game by establishing a science of cybersecurity, transitioning research into practice, and bolstering cybersecurity education and training.

With the rapid pace of technological advancement, we are witnessing the tight integration of financial, business, manufacturing, and telecommunications systems into a networked, global society. These interdependencies can lead to vulnerabilities and threats that challenge the security, reliability, and overall trustworthiness of critical infrastructure. The result is a dramatic shift in the size, complexity, and diversity of cyber attacks.

In response to these changing threats, NSF has long supported fundamental cybersecurity research resulting in many powerful approaches deployed today. NSF continuously brings the problem-solving capabilities of the nation's best minds to bear on these challenges. It also promotes connections between academia and industry.

In Fiscal Year 2014 NSF invested $158.28 million in cybersecurity research, including $126 million in the cross-cutting Secure and Trustworthy Cyberspace program. Projects range from security at the foundational level, including detecting whether a silicon chip contains a malicious circuit or developing new cryptographic solutions, to the systems level, including strategies for securing the electric power grid.

Projects are increasingly interdisciplinary spanning computer science, mathematics, economics, behavioral science, and education. They seek to understand, predict, and explain prevention, attack, and defense behaviors and contribute to developing strategies for remediation while preserving privacy and promoting usability.

Projects also include center scale activities representing far-reaching explorations motivated by deep scientific questions and grand challenge problems in, for example, privacy, encryption, cloud, and healthcare systems.

In addition, NSF promotes the transition of discoveries into the field as threats and solutions co-evolve over time. Partnerships continuously improve the security of our critical infrastructure ensuring U.S. leadership, economic growth, and a skilled workforce. For example, with the Semiconductor Research Corporation, NSF supports research into the design of secure hardware. With Intel Corporation, NSF invests in the security and privacy of cyber-physical systems such as transportation networks and medical devices.

NSF also invests in industry university cooperative research centers that feature high-quality industrially-relevant fundamental research enabling direct transfer of university-developed ideas to U.S. industry, improving its competitiveness globally. In recent years, we have seen research outcomes lead to new products and services and to numerous startups in the IT sector bringing innovative solutions to the marketplace.

Cybersecurity education is also important. For example, the Scholarship for Service program provides tuition to cybersecurity college majors in exchange for government service following graduation. To date, this program has provided 1,700 scholarships at over 50 institutions and has placed graduates in over 140 federal, state, local, and tribal government agencies. NSF participates in the interagency Networking and Information Technology Research and Development program. I serve as the Co-Chair the NITRD Subcommittee and many NSF division directors and program directors actively participate in NITRD cybersecurity and information assurance activities ensuring coordination of investments across 18 government agencies.

To conclude, my testimony today has emphasized that the pace and scope of today's cyber threats pose grand challenges to our nation's critical infrastructure and that NSF continues to make significant investments in fundamental cybersecurity research. I have discussed how NSF partners with industry to advance cybersecurity R&D that will effectively address cyber threats as they evolve.

I very much appreciate the opportunity for dialogue with Members of this Subcommittee on these very important topics. With robust, sustained support for foundational and multidisciplinary cybersecurity R&D in the executive and legislative branches, there is a unique opportunity to protect our national security and enhance our economic prosperity for decades to come.

This concludes my remarks. I am happy to answer any questions.

[The prepared statement of Dr. Kurose follows:]

Testimony of

James F. Kurose, Ph.D.
Assistant Director
Computer and Information Science and Engineering Directorate

Before the
Subcommittee on Research and Technology

For the
Committee on Science, Space, and Technology
U.S. House of Representatives

January 27, 2015

The Expanding Cyber Threat

Good afternoon, Chairwoman, Ranking Member, and members of the Subcommittee. My name is Jim Kurose and I am the National Science Foundation (NSF) Assistant Director for the Computer and Information Science and Engineering Directorate.

As you know, NSF is dedicated to supporting fundamental research in all disciplines, advancing the progress of science and engineering, and educating the next generation of innovative leaders. I welcome this opportunity to highlight NSF's investments in cyber security research and education, including our efforts to work collaboratively with other government agencies and the private sector.

Investments in unclassified, fundamental, long-term research are critical to an effective national strategy for achieving a secure and trustworthy cyberspace. In 2011, NSF contributed to a National Science and Technology Council (NSTC) Strategic Plan titled *Trustworthy Cyberspace: Strategic Plan for the Federal Cybersecurity Research and Development Program*[1]. This plan identifies a broad, coordinated interagency research agenda that focuses on research that "changes the game," minimizes the misuses of cyber technology, bolsters education and training in cyber security, establishes a science of cyber security, and transitions promising research into practice. A major goal is to make cyberspace worthy of the public's trust.

---

[1] http://www.whitehouse.gov/sites/default/files/microsites/ostp/fed_cybersecurity_rd_strategic_plan_2011.pdf

NSF's investments in cyber security are strongly aligned with this Strategic Plan. NSF aims to fund cyber security research at the frontiers of knowledge, to capitalize on the intellectual capacity of both young and experienced investigators in our Nation's academic and research institutions, and to promote connections between academia and industry; collectively, these activities will help to protect cyberspace, secure the Nation's critical infrastructure, and fuel job growth in the decades ahead.

Just as many powerful information technologies (IT) deployed today capitalize on fundamental research outcomes generated decades ago with NSF funding, NSF is bringing the problem-solving capabilities of the Nation's best and brightest minds to bear on the cyber security challenges of today and tomorrow. Let me share with you some examples of the important contributions made in recent years by the cyber security research community with both NSF and other federal support:

- Formal methods and software analyses that further the science of security and privacy via principled techniques for the specification, design and analysis of security mechanisms to secure software programs, and for formalizing and enforcing privacy and accountability in web- and cloud-based systems;
- Protections against vulnerabilities in hardware and product supply chains with new approaches for Trojan detection; protections against counterfeiting of integrated circuits and new tamper-resistant security primitives for hardware;
- Cryptographic schemes and cryptographic-based authentication that enable us to perform computations on encrypted data on untrusted platforms (e.g., on distributed "cloud" platforms);
- Breakthroughs in cryptographic program obfuscation that make it possible to mask the inner workings of a computer program, so that people can use the program without being able to figure out how it works;
- Clean-slate approaches and verifiable operating system kernels that protect traditional desktop and server operating systems and browsers, mobile devices, cloud-based systems, and applications;
- Secure network architectures designed to prevent and mitigate distributed denial-of-service attacks on the Internet, and jamming attacks in wireless communications;
- Identification and protection against security threats to Cyber-Physical Systems (CPS), which include critical infrastructure, via approaches for securing intelligent transportation systems, and anomaly detection in smart grids;
- Innovative machine learning and data mining approaches used in the development of defenses against spam suitable for social networks, and methods for detecting attacks, such as those involving credit card fraud;
- Differential privacy techniques that aim to provide actionable global, statistical information about sensitive data, while preserving the privacy of the users whose information is contained in the data set; and
- Usable security and privacy measures that explore ways to improve warning messages, privacy settings, security interfaces and primitives based on the how end users intuitively respond to such stimuli.

These research innovations and outcomes developed with funding from NSF and other federal partners are now being used by the private sector and government agencies to protect the Nation's critical infrastructure. Moreover, as I will describe later in my testimony, NSF is pioneering multi-disciplinary, collaborative research programs in cyber security across its directorates and with industry. For example, with the Semiconductor Research Corporation (SRC), NSF currently supports research into the design of secure and resilient semiconductors. With Intel Corporation, NSF invests in the security and privacy of cyber-physical systems, such as transportation systems and medical devices. In recent years, research outcomes have led to the formation of numerous start-up companies in the IT sector and the take-up of new products and services that collectively bring innovative solutions to the marketplace and help to protect cyberspace.

The Cyber Security Challenge

While the advances in cyber security research and development (R&D) are many, including those mentioned above, the Nation needs to continue its investments in game-changing research if our cyber systems are to be trustworthy now and in the future. As you know, every day, we learn about more sophisticated and dangerous attacks. Why is the cyber security challenge so hard? The general answer is that attacks and defenses co-evolve: a system that was secure yesterday might no longer be secure tomorrow. More specific responses to this question include:

- The technology base of our critical infrastructure systems is frequently updated to improve functionality, availability, and/or performance. New systems introduce new vulnerabilities (unknowable in the lab) that need new defenses when put into practice.
- The environments in which our computing systems are rapidly developed and deployed, and the functionality that they provide are also not static. With entirely new computing models/platforms, like cloud and mobile computing, come new content and function, which in turn create new opportunities and incentives for attack and disruption.
- As the automation of complex system interdependencies comes to pervade our critical infrastructure, new kinds of cascading vulnerabilities can be accidentally created and subsequently discovered in these systems, including the electric power grid, automated transportation networks, and robotic medical systems.
- The sophistication of attackers is increasing as well as their sheer number and the specificity of their targets.
- As information and systems are increasingly connected, and are increasingly composed of software and hardware produced by global supply chains, the opportunities for malicious insiders to cause damage increases, and the risks of information leaks multiply.
- As more systems and data become accessible, information that was once low risk becomes high risk through correlation that was unimaginable only a few years ago.
- Achieving system trustworthiness is not purely a technology problem. System developers, purchasers, operators and users all have a role to play in system security, and ways to incentivize positive behaviors are required. Security mechanisms that are not convenient will be circumvented; security mechanisms that are difficult to understand will be ignored or misinterpreted. Indeed, cyber security is a multi-dimensional challenge, requiring expertise in computer science, mathematics, economics, behavioral sciences, and education.

Emerging Threats

With the rapid pace of technological advancement, daily life is now intimately connected to the Internet. Key aspects of business operations, our financial systems, manufacturing supply chains, and military communications are tightly networked, integrating the economic, political, and social fabric of our global society. As I discussed previously, these interdependencies can lead to vulnerabilities and a wide range of threats that challenge the security, reliability, availability, and overall trustworthiness of all systems and resources rooted in information technology. Coupled with Internet adoption patterns, we are witnessing a dramatic shift in the size, complexity, and diversity of cyber security attacks. Let me expand upon four key technology and adoption trends:

- The proliferation of mobile devices and wireless networks exposes new vulnerabilities;
- The protection of "cloud" infrastructure has become key to long-term adoption;
- Increasingly, cyber-enabled systems expand the scope of attacks to physical infrastructure, including critical infrastructure in domains such as manufacturing, energy production and consumption, healthcare, and transportation; and
- Social media platforms open new avenues for hackers.

The number of mobile devices has soared in the last several years; there are already more mobile devices connected to the Internet than tethered devices. By the year 2018, analysts expect the number of mobile-connected devices to be 10 billion, or nearly one and one-half times the world's population[2]. Mobile devices are increasingly characterized by their pervasiveness and connectedness: they have eclipsed traditional computers as points of entry to the Internet in an era of "always-on, always-connected" communications. Smartphones and tablets are able to access data in a wide variety of forms, from text messaging to web browsing to live applications ("apps") for streaming services, gaming, and beyond. Moreover, apps are taking advantage of a user's presence in time and space, and combined with other relevant data, are delivering targeted and tailored content and services. The result is a future that is increasingly smart and connected. Hundreds of thousands of applications available today support banking, e-commerce, highway navigation, health and wellbeing, and social networking, for example; the future will only bring more varied applications used in all facets of daily life.

The current culture that encourages application downloading makes mobile devices especially vulnerable to malware. For example, a recent study found that mobile device malware rates – reflecting the number of devices attacked but not infected – surged 75 percent from 2013 to 2014 alone, often through downloadable software masquerading as something else[3]. The natural desire to accomplish a task, whether business or pleasure, leads to clicking "yes" in response to online requests, which in turn enables further compromise of our systems. NSF-funded research is exploring solutions, including better understanding of the mobile app ecosystem, crowd-based advice for whether a mobile app has security or privacy risks, personality-driven user interfaces, and understanding how the brain intuitively senses messages.

Additionally, with cloud computing and the proliferation of mobile devices, an organization's information is no longer stored and accessed within its walls or perimeters. Information is frequently entirely created and stored in the "cloud." Systems and resources, including networks, hosts, storage, data centers and applications, are increasingly virtualized and distributed, and commonly under the control of the cloud service providers and the end-users themselves. Confidential information and intellectual property are increasingly flowing from back-end systems that the organization doesn't own or fully control, through networks that it doesn't own or control, to endpoints and end-users that it doesn't fully control. This evolution toward the cloud requires continued research and development; new approaches for protecting cloud infrastructure will be key to its long-term success. Side-channel attacks on cloud infrastructure, allowing an observer in the cloud to observe side effects of what other cloud users are doing, allow inferences that were not possible in pre-cloud environments. The National

---

[2] http://www.cisco.com/c/en/us/solutions/collateral/service-provider/visual-networking-index-vni/white_paper_c11-520862.html
[3] http://www.cnbc.com/id/102338872#.

Institute of Standards and Technology's definition of, and recommendations for, cloud computing[4] provide additional information. NSF investments in cloud computing security have been summarized in annual reports[5].

Computers are embedded everywhere, from the cash register in the coffee shop to sensors in highways, actuators in medical devices, and controls in manufacturing plants. As these systems are increasingly connected to the Internet, the threat landscape continues to evolve. The Target breach of 2013-2014 showed the risks of interconnected systems, with the initial compromise through an HVAC contractor[6]. Remote access to cash registers has been used to steal credit card numbers, as may have been the case in breaches affecting Home Depot[7] and over 1,000 other U.S. merchants[8]. As I will describe later in my testimony, NSF-funded researchers have demonstrated the ability to gain wireless access to a combination heart defibrillator and pacemaker, and are now working with colleagues in industry on security engineering of medical devices and implants.

Risks include privacy as well as security. Tire pressure sensors installed to help drivers avoid dangerous tire under- or over-inflation can be remotely identified, thus allowing a stalker to inconspicuously track movements of potential victims or allowing criminals to track undercover law enforcement officers around a city. Beyond computer virus infections that have disabled operating room computers, hospitals have been victim to breaches of patient records. Recent studies show that a large fraction of hospital equipment is vulnerable to computer attacks[9].

Deliberate and seemingly reasonable security measures can also backfire. GoGo Inflight, which provides WiFi access on airplanes, replaces digital certificates used to prove the identity of websites with its own certificates[10], allowing it to decrypt network traffic and prevent video streaming that would interfere with throughput for other passengers. As a side effect, however, sensitive email traffic could be decrypted before it leaves the airplane, and then re-encrypted, introducing risks for executives who are the most likely to use airplane wireless services. Attackers could employ the same strategy by placing open "hotspots" at coffee shops. While such a cyber threat is easily detectable and circumvented, it requires technical understanding by users who are used to clicking "yes" to messages.

In light of these challenges, the Nation's cyber security research community is key to enabling the design, implementation, and deployment of systems that are secure and trustworthy. NSF continues to formulate and develop a comprehensive research portfolio around a view of systems that are deemed *trustworthy*, i.e., systems that people can depend on day after day and year after year to operate correctly and safely – from our avionics, mass transit and automobile systems to medical devices operated remotely to save lives on battlefields. Included in this notion of trustworthiness are a number of critical concepts: *reliability* (does it work as intended?); *security* (how vulnerable is it to attack?); *privacy* (does it protect a person's information?); and *usability* (can a human easily use it?). Research needs to be game-changing and forward-looking; new policies and continued focus on cyber security education, public awareness and workforce development are critical to our success.

Four principles guide NSF's investments in cyber security research:

---

[4] http://csrc.nist.gov/publications/nistpubs/800-145/SP800-145.pdf
[5] http://www.nsf.gov/pubs/2012/nsf12040/nsf12040.pdf
[6] http://krebsonsecurity.com/2014/02/target-hackers-broke-in-via-hvac-company/
[7] http://bits.blogs.nytimes.com/2014/09/18/home-depot-says-data-from-56-million-cards-taken-in-breach/?_r=0
[8] http://www.hngn.com/articles/40068/20140823/cash-register-hack-affected-over-1-000-u-s-businesses.htm
[9] http://www.wired.com/2014/04/hospital-equipment-vulnerable/
[10] http://arstechnica.com/security/2015/01/gogo-issues-fake-https-certificate-to-users-visiting-youtube/

- Uncover and address the underlying cyber security research gaps by focusing on the root causes of cyber security challenges rather than just treating the symptoms;
- Develop a "science of security" based on enduring cyber security principles that will allow us to stay secure despite challenges in technology and the evolution of new threat environments;
- Approach cyber security as a multi-dimensional challenge, involving both the strengths of security technologies and the variability of human behavior; and
- Enable the "right science and engineering at the right scale" by casting a wide net that encourages more speculative research, and multiple perspectives including accelerating the transitioning of research results into practice.

Given this summary of the emerging threats in cyber security and NSF's contributions to these challenges, let me now turn to the issues that were raised by the Subcommittee in the invitation to this hearing.

(1) Provide an overview of the research the National Science Foundation (NSF) supports related to cyberinfrastructure, risk management, threat detection, identity management, and other issues related to cyber security.

As stated in its organic act, NSF's mission is "to promote the progress of science; to advance the national health, prosperity, and welfare; to secure the national defense…" Support for basic and applied research is integral to NSF's mission.

Cyber Security R&D Portfolio

NSF has been investing in cyber security research for many years. In FY 2014, NSF invested $158.28 million in unclassified, fundamental, long-term research in the science of trustworthiness and related trustworthy systems and technologies. Today, NSF's cyber security research portfolio includes projects addressing security from the microscopic level, detecting whether a silicon chip is a counterfeit or may contain a malicious circuit, to the macroscopic level, determining strategies for securing the next-generation electrical power grid and transportation network, as well as at the human level, studying online privacy and security behaviors of both adolescents and senior citizens, methods for leveraging personality differences to improve security behaviors, and understanding motivations for keeping systems patched. Fundamental research in cryptography, cryptographic protocol analysis, formal specification and verification techniques, static and dynamic program analysis, and security testing methods contribute to improved methods for building socio-technical systems that perform as intended, even in the face of threats. Research in calculating on encrypted data will allow for secure cloud computation; methods for executing encrypted software will provably prevent adversaries from reverse engineering software to find vulnerabilities that can be exploited. Research in secure programming languages and methodologies, and in securing operating systems and especially the virtualization mechanisms and hypervisors on which much of the security of cloud computing architectures depends is also prominent in NSF's portfolio. NSF's researchers are investigating novel methods for detecting when security measures have failed, when intrusions have occurred, and when information may have been altered or stolen. NSF's portfolio includes projects studying security in human-centric systems and in a variety of web-application contexts as well as in smartphones, voting systems, medical devices, automotive systems, and other cyber-physical systems. New methods explore how to effectively communicate security and privacy information to users in ways that they can better understand, and offer approaches for blind users to receive useful but unobtrusive security information, since "pop up" warnings are ineffective. Collaborations between computer scientists and social scientists continue to expand the scope of how we understand security problems and their solutions.

Across NSF's portfolio of cyber security research, about a third of the investments are in projects that involve one to two faculty researchers and one to two graduate students, and another are in projects that involve small teams of researchers, including graduate students. Here are some specific examples of the kinds of foundational research projects that small teams of researchers are pursuing, and their intended broader significance:

- Integrated circuits used in all forms of electronics are subject to counterfeits, which may violate intellectual property laws, be less reliable, or even dangerous. This research develops mechanisms that can tell if a chip is new or used, and discern genuine from counterfeit chips in a method similar to a car's Vehicle Identification Number (VIN) and odometer.
- Internet traffic can be redirected through alternate locations, akin to redirecting vehicles through a neighborhood by posting "Detour" signs. This technique has been used for potentially nefarious purposes, including a 2013 attack that sent U.S. Internet traffic through a foreign country. Ongoing research is developing new methods to improve the ability to detect such redirections and characterize their extent, frequency, and impact, and share summary reports with network operators, emergency response teams, law enforcement, and policy makers.
- Voting systems must meet a wide range of requirements, including cost, accuracy, resilience against attack, auditability, and usability by all citizens who are infrequent voters. An NSF award in collaboration with the government of Travis County, TX, seeks to create voting systems that can address all of these needs simultaneously, building on the past decade of research on risks to voting technology.
- Biometric approaches, such as fingerprinting and iris recognition, hold tremendous promise to prove identity to computer systems, but still have significant limitations, including susceptibility to "spoofing." An NSF-funded research team is seeking to advance our knowledge of security and accuracy of "multi-biometric" systems by inventing, evaluating, and applying innovative methods and tools to combine highly accurate static traits, such as iris patterns, with novel traits based on the dynamics of eye movements that cannot be spoofed. These techniques do not require new hardware, and can be used for other purposes beyond identification such as discerning fatigue or concussion.
- When a photograph is shared online through social media, the person sharing the photo (usually the photographer) makes decisions about who can see it, rather than the people whose images are in the photo. Ongoing research aims to address technical methods for allowing people to control how privacy protections can protect their images.

Beyond single-investigator and team awards, NSF also invests in center-scale activities. Since 2012, the Secure and Trustworthy Computing program has funded seven center-scale projects called "frontiers," representing far-reaching explorations motivated by deep scientific questions and grand challenge problems in security, privacy, encryption, cloud computing, and healthcare systems, to name a few:

- *Beyond Technical Security: Developing an Empirical Basis for Socio-Economic Perspectives* at the University of California at San Diego, University of California at Berkeley, and George Mason University (2012) – This research tackles the technical and economic elements of Internet security: how the motivations and interactions of attackers, defenders and users shape the threats we face, how they evolve over time and how they can best be addressed. This research has the potential to dramatically benefit society by undermining entire cybercrime ecosystems by, for example, disrupting underground activities, infrastructure and social networks.

- *Privacy Tools for Sharing Research Data* at Harvard University (2012) – A multi-disciplinary team of researchers is developing tools and policies to aid in the collection, analysis and sharing of data in cyberspace, while protecting individual privacy. The ideas and tools developed in this project will have a significant broad impact on society since the issues addressed in the work arise in many other important domains, including public health and electronic commerce.

- *Enabling Trustworthy Cybersystems for Health and Wellness* at Dartmouth University, the University of Illinois at Urbana-Champaign, Johns Hopkins University, and University of Michigan at Ann Arbor (2013) – This interdisciplinary center investigates ways to provide trustworthy information systems for health and wellness in the context of sensitive information and health-related tasks being increasingly pushed into mobile devices and cloud-based services. In the long term, this project will help create mobile health systems that can be trusted by individual citizens to protect their privacy and by health professionals to ensure data integrity and security.

- *Rethinking Security in the Era of Cloud Computing* at the University of North Carolina at Chapel Hill, Stony Brook University, Duke University, North Carolina State University, and University of Wisconsin at Madison (2013) – This project explores ways of improving security of data and services in the cloud by addressing key challenges like secure transport, authorization, user and software authentication and security monitoring. This project challenges the common perception that the cloud decreases security for its customers, and instead envisions new opportunities for improving the security of data and services by moving them to the cloud.

- *Towards Effective Web Privacy Notice and Choice: A Multi-disciplinary Perspective* at Carnegie Mellon University, Fordham University, and Stanford University (2013) – This project explores ways to improve the usability of privacy policies by developing scalable technologies to semi-automatically extract key privacy policy features from website privacy policies, and presenting these features to users in an easy-to-digest format akin to nutrition labels on food products. This research will enable Internet users to make informed privacy decisions as they contemplate interacting with different websites.

- *Center for Encrypted Functionalities* at the University of California at Los Angeles, Stanford University, Columbia University, University of Texas at Austin, and Johns Hopkins University (2014) – This project explores new encryption methods to make a computer program, and not just its output, invisible to an outside observer, while preserving its functionality – a process known as program obfuscation. Members of this team recently discovered the first mathematically sound approach to encrypting functionalities – a breakthrough could reshape the way we think about security and computation.

- *Modular Approach to Cloud Security* at Boston University, the Massachusetts Institute of Technology, University of Connecticut, and Northeastern University (2014) – This project aims to investigate, design and test a modular approach to cyber security for cloud systems, with the aim of addressing the question of how the security of the system as a whole can be derived from the security of its components. The project has the potential to transform the way we build and reason about information systems with meaningful multi-layered security.

NSF aims to provide high-level visibility to grand challenge research areas in cyber security by enabling such center-scale activities that bring together interdisciplinary expertise from multiple institutions to focus in-depth on topics of national importance.

Cyber Security Programs

The discussion above focused on the different scales of NSF-funded cyber security research. Let me now take a programmatic view of these activities. The National Science Foundation funds a broad range of activities to advance cyber security research, develop a well-educated and capable workforce, and to keep all citizens informed and aware. FY 2015 investments in these activities include $126 million in the Secure and Trustworthy Cyberspace (SaTC) program, led by the Directorate for Computer and Information Science and Engineering (CISE) in partnership with the Directorates for Education and Human Resources (EHR), Engineering, Mathematical and Physical Sciences, and Social, Behavioral, and Economic Sciences. Currently, there are over 670 Secure and Trustworthy Cyberspace awards that are active, including 175 new research projects in 35 states that were funded in FY 2014 alone.

To provide some context about NSF's Secure and Trustworthy Cyberspace program, since FY 2012[11], this program has sought to secure the Nation's cyberspace by addressing two perspectives within the multi-dimensional cyber security problem space:

* *Trustworthy computing systems*, with goals to provide the basis for designing, building, and operating a cyberinfrastructure with improved resistance and improved resilience to attack, and that can be tailored to meet a wide range of technical and policy requirements, including both privacy and accountability.
* *Social, behavioral and economic sciences*, with goals to understand, predict, and explain prevention, attack and/or defense behaviors and contribute to developing strategies for remediation. Research that contributes to the design of incentives, markets, or institutions to reduce either the likelihood of cyber-attack or the negative consequences of cyber-attack are especially encouraged, as are projects that examine incentives and motivations of individuals.

In FY 2013, the Secure and Trustworthy Cyberspace program began addressing a third perspective on *cyber security education,* with the goal to promote innovation, development, and assessment of new learning opportunities and to create and sustain an unrivaled cyber security workforce capable of developing secure cyberinfrastructure components and systems, as well as to raise the awareness of cyber security challenges to a more general population.

In FY 2015, the Secure and Trustworthy Cyberspace program has started explicitly addressing a fourth perspective, *Secure, Trustworthy, Assured and Resilient Semiconductors and Systems (STARSS)*, with the goal to develop strategies, techniques and tools that avoid and mitigate hardware vulnerabilities and lead to semiconductors and systems that are resistant and resilient to attack or tampering. STARSS is a joint effort of NSF and the Semiconductor Research Corporation (SRC), as I will describe later in my testimony.

Beyond these four perspectives, the Secure and Trustworthy Cyberspace program aims to address the challenge of moving from research to capability. The program supports research activities whose outcomes are capable of being implemented, applied, experimentally used, or deployed in an

---

[11] NSF has been investing in cyber security research for many years, including through the Trusted Computing (FY 2002-2003), Cyber Trust (FY 2004-2008), and Trustworthy Computing (FY 2009-2011) programs. Beginning in FY 2012, the Secure and Trustworthy Cyberspace program has aligned NSF's investments with the 2011 federal Strategic Plan, *Trustworthy Cyberspace: Strategic Plan for the Federal Cybersecurity Research and Development Program*. Since 2002, NSF has issued over 1,700 cyber security awards.

operational environment. Such efforts can result in fielded capabilities and innovations of direct benefit to networks, systems, and environments supporting NSF science and engineering research and education communities. Areas of emphasis for these "transition to practice" investments have included malware detection and prevention, situational understanding, data assurance, risk analysis, and software assurance.

In addition to the Secure and Trustworthy Cyberspace program, NSF continues to make cyber security investments in the core scientific sub-disciplines of: the computing and information sciences, including the foundations of algorithms and information and communications sciences, cyber-physical systems, smart health and wellbeing, future internet architectures, networking technology and systems, information integration and informatics; the social, behavioral, and economic sciences, including an understanding of market forces and social/cognitive factors associated with developing secure, trustworthy systems; engineering, including the development of advanced cyber security algorithms that can integrate with hardware architectures to improve the security of the Nation's critical communications, electric power, health, and financial information systems; and the mathematical and physical sciences, including the foundations of cryptographic, statistical, topological, and graph-based methods and algorithms, as well as risk analysis and assessments to address challenges in cyber security.

NSF's support of cyber security research includes a focus on privacy. In FY 2014, NSF invested about $25 million to support privacy research as an extension of security, including exploring basic privacy constructs and their application in many areas of information technology. NSF's privacy support is largely driven bottom-up by research proposals from the academic research community.

Indeed, across its cyber security research and development programs, NSF continues to cast a wide net and let the best ideas surface, rather than pursuing a prescriptive research agenda. It engages the cyber security research community in developing new fundamental, long-term, often interdisciplinary or multi-disciplinary ideas, which are evaluated by the best researchers through the merit review process. This process, which supports the vast majority of unclassified cyber security research in the U.S., has led to innovative and transformative results, some of which I have previously described in my testimony.

(2) Why is NSF supported research important to individuals and industry?

(3) What impact does NSF research have on the cyber-industry, including critical infrastructure?

Allow me to answer these two questions below.

As part of its cyber security investments, NSF promotes partnerships between academia and industry. These are critical to a healthy trustworthy computing ecosystem. They enable discoveries to transition out of the lab and into the field as threats and solutions co-evolve over time. And they ensure U.S. leadership, economic growth, and a skilled workforce.

Specifically, NSF envisions a thriving research community that will address major technological challenges for the next generation of devices and systems, including the security and trustworthiness of these devices and systems. As part of this effort, NSF supports fundamental research underlying device and component technologies, power, controls, computation, networking, communications and cyber technologies. NSF supports the integration and networking of intelligent systems principles at the nano-, micro-, and macro-scales for a variety of application domains spanning healthcare, homeland security, disaster mitigation, energy, telecommunications, environment, transportation, manufacturing, and other systems-related areas.

NSF has therefore worked closely with the Semiconductor Research Corporation (SRC), the world's leading technology research consortium consisting of member companies and university research programs across the globe, in the area of hardware security. Through the Secure, Trustworthy, Assured, and Resilient Semiconductors and Systems (STARSS) perspective within the Secure and Trustworthy Cyberspace program, NSF and SRC are funding innovations in hardware security and facilitating close collaborations between academic researchers and industry.

Computing processors meet a huge range of needs, from leading-edge processors that are the "brains" behind critically-important systems and infrastructure, including networking and communications, electric power grids, finance, military, and aerospace systems, to smaller embedded processors, sensors, and other electronic components that provide "smart" functionality and connectivity in a variety of applications, such as automotive braking and airbag systems, personal healthcare, industrial controls, and the rapidly growing list of connected devices often called the "Internet of Things" (IoT). The wide range of devices and applications together with the exponential growth of the number of connected "things" has made security and trustworthiness a prime concern.

Design and manufacture of today's complex hardware systems requires many steps and involves the work of hundreds of engineers, typically distributed across multiple locations and organizations worldwide. Today, semiconductor circuits and systems are designed so as to make it feasible or easier to verify, manufacture and test during subsequent steps. However, what is needed is an understanding of how to design for assurance, with the objective of decreasing the likelihood of unintended behavior or access, increasing resistance and resilience to tampering and counterfeiting, and improving the ability to provide authentication in the field. Designing for assurance requires new strategies for architecture and specification, and tools for synthesis, physical design, test, and verification, especially at the stages of design in which formal methods are currently weak or absent. It is imperative to develop a theoretical basis for hardware security in order to design systems that are free of vulnerability and that are assured and resilient against attacks, even vulnerabilities and attacks that are not (yet) known. Through our partnership, NSF and SRC jointly funded nine projects in FY 2014 spanning these areas, with additional awards anticipated in FY 2015.

NSF is also partnering with Intel Corporation in the area of cyber-physical systems, security and privacy. The national and economic security of the U.S. depends on the reliable function of critical infrastructure. This infrastructure is rapidly being advanced through the integration of information and communication technologies, leading to cyber-physical systems. Advances in CPS will enable capability, adaptability, scalability, and usability that will far exceed the simple embedded systems of today. CPS technologies will transform the way people interact with engineered systems – just as the Internet has transformed the way people interact with information. New smart CPS will drive innovation and competition in sectors such as food and agriculture, energy, different modes of transportation including air and automobiles, building design and automation, healthcare and medical implants, and advanced manufacturing.

Cyber-physical systems are subject to threats stemming from increasing reliance on computer and communication technologies. Cyber security threats exploit the increased complexity and connectivity of critical infrastructure systems, placing the Nation's security, economy, public safety, and health at risk.

The goal of our partnership with Intel is to foster novel, transformative, multidisciplinary approaches that ensure the security of current and emerging cyber-physical systems, taking into consideration the unique challenges present in this environment relative to other domains with cyber security concerns. These challenges arise from the non-reversible nature of the interactions of CPS with the physical world; the scale of deployment; the federated nature of numerous infrastructures; the deep embedding and long projected lifetimes of CPS components; the interaction of CPS with users at different scales, degrees of control, and expertise levels; the economic and policy constraints under which such systems must often operate; and the sensing and collection of information related to a large spectrum of everyday human activities. The first set of joint NSF/Intel awards are planned for FY 2015.

NSF has also invested in two active Industry/University Cooperative Research Centers (I/UCRCs), which feature high-quality, industrially relevant fundamental research, strong industrial support of and collaboration in research and education, and direct transfer of university-developed ideas, research results, and technology to U.S. industry to improve its competitive posture in world markets. I/UCRCs, in general, are a great investment in the future. Across the I/UCRC program, over 2,000 students were supported in 2014, with 649 attaining their degrees, including 185 students who were hired directly by industrial members of their I/UCRCs. On average, I/UCRCs saw a six to one leveraging of NSF funds in 2014. The two cyber security-related centers are:

- *CITeR: Center for Identification Technology Research (Biometrics)* at Clarkson University, the University of Arizona, West Virginia University, University of Buffalo, and Michigan State University – CITeR aims to advance understanding in biometrics and credibility assessment central to realization of next generation identification management systems necessary for private sector and government applications. CITeR's research includes iris, fingerprint, face, voice, and gait recognition, and will significantly enhance the research database available for the disciplines involved with security biometrics technologies. Research is needed in large-scale, fully-automated, distributed systems in several application areas, ranging from driver's licenses to passports and visas, for example.
- *S2ERC: Security and Software Engineering* at Ball State University, Iowa State University, Virginia Tech, and Georgetown University – S2ERC investigates integrated methods of engineering practical software systems that are able to meet emerging security requirements. This goal is important to both industry and government in order for them to confidently deploy real-world software systems that meet their mission goals in the face of a broad range of security attacks. Recent S2ERC research projects have focused on software design, metrics, testing, and reliability in the face of intrusion detection, ad-hoc network security, wireless security, attack-tolerant systems, and trustworthiness in cloud and mobile applications.

Beyond these academic/industry collaborations, a critical aspect of the SaTC program for all research projects is the Transition to Practice, or TTP, option, which supports proposed research activities and ideas whose outcomes at the end of the award are capable of being implemented, applied, experimentally used, or deployed in an operational environment. Transitioning research into practice, whether in research programs, commercial products, or use in government agencies shortens the time from ideas to practical solutions.

NSF is also co-funding "Innovation Transitions" (InTrans) awards with industry partners for cyber security research teams at the point of completing their center-scale projects, with the goals of continuing the long-term vision and objectives of the project team, maturing and deploying successful research and innovation results in industry, and facilitating the transition of the innovations to support from industrial sponsors with the potential to develop new technologies.

NSF-funded cyber security research has also led to the formation of numerous start-up companies in the IT sector and the take-up of new products and services, all of which bring innovative solutions to the marketplace, spurring job growth and helping to protect cyberspace. NSF has supported these start-ups through specific programs, including:

- The Small Business Innovation Research (SBIR) and Small Business Technology Transfer (STTR) programs stimulate technological innovation in the private sector by strengthening the role of small business concerns in meeting federal research and development needs, increasing the commercial application of federally supported research results, and fostering and encouraging participation by socially and economically disadvantaged and women-owned small businesses. Outcomes of several NSF-funded cyber security research projects have led to NSF SBIR and STTR grants.
- The NSF Innovation Corps™ (I-Corps™) is a public-private partnership that teaches grantees to identify valuable product opportunities that emerge from academic research, and offers entrepreneurship training to student participants. Since the inception of the NSF Innovation Corps™ program in 2011, a number of I-Corps™ Teams in the cyber security domain have participated in the I-Corps™ curriculum.

Finally, a number of NSF-funded researchers, particularly those working in larger, inter- or multidisciplinary teams, collaborate closely with industry to deepen and extend the outcomes of their research activities. For example, NSF-funded researchers at the University of California at San Diego and University of Washington have demonstrated the ability to remotely take over automotive control systems[12]. The researchers found that, because many of today's cars contain cellular connections and Bluetooth wireless technology, it is possible for a hacker working from a remote location to take control of various features – like the car locks and brakes – as well as to track the vehicle's location, eavesdrop on its passenger cabin, and steal vehicle data. The researchers are now working with the automotive industry to develop new methods for assuring the safety and security of on-board electronics. Both the Society for Automotive Engineers (SAE) and the United States Council for Automotive Research (USCAR) have partnered with the researchers to stand up efforts focused on automotive security research[13]. Automotive manufacturers have also started dedicating significant resources to security[14].

Similarly, NSF-funded researchers at the University of Michigan, University of Massachusetts Amherst, and University of Washington were able to gain wireless access to a combination heart defibrillator and pacemaker, reprogramming it to shut it down and to deliver jolts of electricity that could have potentially been fatal if the device had been implanted in a person. This research team is now collaborating with industry, including the Medical Device Innovation, Safety, and Security (MDISS) Consortium, Association for the Advancement of Medical Instrumentation (AAMI), and specific biomedical device companies, including Medtronic, Philips Healthcare, Siemens Healthcare, and Welch Allyn, to prevent illegal or unauthorized hacking of devices that have wireless capabilities. For each of the last two years, this NSF-funded research team has also held a Medical Device Security Workshop[15,16] to bring together solution-oriented experts in medical device manufacturing and computer security to meet and discuss effective ways to improve information security and inform Food and Drug Administration (FDA) guidelines on cyber security. Additionally, the research team has created a

---

[12] http://www.nytimes.com/2011/03/10/business/10hack.html
[13] http://www.autosec.org/faq.html
[14] http://www.caranddriver.com/features/can-your-car-be-hacked-feature
[15] http://secure-medicine.org/workshop/2014
[16] http://secure-medicine.org/workshop/2013

traveling classroom for medical device manufacturers, and has provided private on-site security engineering education and training to over 500 employees from a half-dozen major medical device manufacturers. We expect such academic/industry collaborations to continue to grow as new cyber security challenges and results emerge.

Education and Workforce Development

NSF's investments in cyber security research are accompanied by investments in cyber security education and workforce development. Research undertaken in academia not only engages some of our nation's best and brightest researchers, but because these researchers are also teachers, new generations of students are exposed to the latest thinking from the people who understand it best. And when these students graduate and move into the workplace, they will bring this knowledge and understanding with them. Moreover, faculty members in this dual role of researchers and teachers have incentives to write textbooks and prepare other teaching materials that allow dissemination of their work to a wide audience, including teachers and students nationwide.

Supporting the Next Generation of Cyber Security Researchers

In recent years, through the Research Experiences for Undergraduates (REU) program, NSF has supported several REU Sites based on independent proposals that seek to initiate and conduct projects that engage a number of undergraduate students in research. REU Sites must have a well-defined common focus, based in a single discipline or spanning interdisciplinary or multi-disciplinary research opportunities with a coherent intellectual theme, which enables a cohort experience for students. Each REU Site typically supports 8 to 12 undergraduate students each summer, including housing and stipend support, with each student involved in a specific project guided by a faculty mentor. REU Sites are an important means for extending high-quality research environments and mentoring to diverse groups of students. NSF's investments in REU Sites focused on cyber security and information assurance include:

- *Trustable Computing Systems Security Research and Education* at the University of Connecticut;
- *Information Assurance and Security* at Dakota State University;
- *Undergraduates Engaged in Cyber Security Research* at the University of Maryland;
- *Site for Extensive and Collaborative Undergraduate Research Experience (SECURE)* at the University of Nebraska at Omaha;
- *Multidisciplinary Information Assurance and Security* at Purdue University; and
- *Digital Forensics Research in Rhode Island* at the University of Rhode Island.

Over the years, the Secure and Trustworthy Cyberspace program has supplemented its awards by providing small amounts of additional funding to researchers to bring undergraduates into their labs throughout the school year through the REU program. This program gives many undergraduate students their first hands-on experiences with real science and engineering research projects. In addition, through the REU mechanism, the Secure and Trustworthy Cyberspace program has supplemented awards to provide research experiences for teachers in computer science and engineering, as well as for U.S. veterans who wish to engage in meaningful research experiences, as recommended by the April 2009 report of an NSF-funded workshop on *Veterans' Education for Engineering and Science*[17].

---

[17] http://www.nsf.gov/eng/eec/VeteranEducation.pdf

The Secure and Trustworthy Cyberspace program has provided awards to support travel and accommodations for students who wish to attend premier research conferences and workshops in information assurance and cyber security. Each award provides funding for 10 to 20 full-time students attending accredited institutions, who in turn can attend conferences and workshops to present their research, learn about advances in the field, and meet prospective colleagues and collaborators. SaTC student travel grant awardees encourage women and other underrepresented minorities to apply for these funds.

The Secure and Trustworthy Cyberspace program has also funded young investigators through the CAREER program that offers NSF's most prestigious awards in support of junior faculty who exemplify the role of teacher-scholars through outstanding research, excellent education and the integration of education and research within the context of the mission of their organizations.

	FY 2012	FY 2013	FY 2014
SaTC CAREER awards	14	13	9
SaTC REU Sites and Supplements	34	32	42
SaTC conference student travel awards	11	15	15

Nurturing and Growing the Cyber Security PI Community

Additionally, the Secure and Trustworthy Cyberspace program has sought to broaden the cyber security research community, which is critical to facilitating advances in the field. For example, in FY 2013 and FY 2014, the program organized and held Aspiring SaTC Principal Investigators (PIs) workshops that sought to educate potential cyber security researchers on the priorities of the program and components of successful research projects. NSF plans to continue to use this approach to bring new researchers with a broad set of talents and interests into the SaTC PI community.

The program has also held biennial meetings of all its PIs, including most recently in FY 2013 and FY 2015. These meetings have sought to bring PIs together with representatives from academe, industry, and government, with the goals of understanding progress and identifying emerging research challenges; fostering collaboration and coordination among PIs, both within and across specific science and engineering disciplines; sharing experiences and learning from others' experiences in transitioning research into practice; and understanding strategies and methods for improving education, recruitment, and career development in cyber security.

Training for Cyber Security Professionals

Beyond the growth of the cyber security research and education community, the NSF Directorate for Education and Human Resources (EHR) has focused on increasing the number of professionals with degrees in cyber security. An overwhelming majority of these EHR-developed professionals were supported by the CyberCorps®: Scholarship for Service (SFS) and/or Advanced Technological Education (ATE) programs.

The SFS program provides funding to colleges and universities for scholarships and capacity building to increase the number of qualified students entering the fields of information assurance and cyber security and to increase the capacity of the higher education enterprise to produce professionals in those fields. The SFS program is an interagency program administered by NSF in collaboration with the Office of Personnel Management (OPM), the Department of Homeland Security (DHS), and the National Security Agency (NSA), among other agencies. SFS was established as a result of a January 2000 Presidential Executive Order that defined the National Plan for Information Systems Protection. The Cybersecurity Enhancement Act of 2014 (Public Law No. 113-274) directs NSF, in coordination with OPM and DHS, to continue the SFS program to recruit and train the next generation of information technology professionals, industrial control system security professionals, and security managers to meet the needs of the cyber security mission for Federal, State, local, and tribal governments. The SFS program supports two tracks.

The Scholarship Track provides funds to colleges and universities to award scholarships to students in support of their education in areas relevant to cyber security. In return for their scholarships, recipients must agree to work after graduation for the federal government or, subject to approval from NSF, for a state, local, or tribal government in a position related to cyber security for a period equal to the length of the scholarship.

During the scholarship period, the students will participate in meaningful summer internships. Doctoral students may be allowed to replace their summer internship with a research activity following a recommendation from their academic advisor and approval of NSF.

To be eligible for consideration for an SFS scholarship, a student must be a U.S. citizen, be within two to three years of graduation in a coherent formal bachelor's, master's, or doctoral program focused on cyber security at an awardee institution, and be able to meet selection criteria for federal employment. Each proposing institution must provide a description of its selection criteria and process, and must submit their lists of candidates for SFS scholarships to OPM for final eligibility confirmation.

Through the end of FY 2014, the SFS program has provided scholarships to more than 2,300 students and graduated more than 1,700, including 22 percent with bachelor's degrees, 76 percent with master's degrees, and two percent with doctoral degrees. Of these graduates, 93 percent have been successfully placed in the Federal government. SFS scholarship recipients have been placed in internships and full-time positions in more than 140 federal departments, agencies, and branches, and state, local, and tribal governments, including the National Security Agency, Department of Homeland Security, Central Intelligence Agency, and Department of Justice.

Graduating Class	
2002	9
2003	75
2004	153
2005	179
2006	172
2007	158
2008	122
2009	86
2010	121
2011	116
2012	175
2013	171
Jan-Sept 2014	170
Total	**1707**

Top 15 Universities (Students Enrolled FY 2009-2014)	
University of Tulsa	98
Carnegie Mellon University	72
Mississippi State University	60
California State University, San Bernardino	58
Northeastern University	42
University of North Carolina at Charlotte	42
Naval Postgraduate School	41
NYU - Polytechnic	40
Idaho State University	39
University of Illinois at Urbana Champaign	38
Air Force Institute of Technology	36
North Carolina A & T State University	35
Dakota State University	34
University of Nebraska at Omaha	28
University of Texas at Dallas	28
Other 38 universities	523
Total	**1240**

Placement FY 2009-14	
National Security Agency	120
US Navy	66
Mitre Corporation	53
Department of Homeland Security	50
Federal Reserve System	35
State, Local, & Tribal	34
Sandia Laboratory	32
Department of Defense	31
Software Engineering Institute	28
Central Intelligence Agency	27
US Air Force	23
US Army	23
Department of Treasury	21
Department of Justice	20
Lincoln Laboratory	20
Other	129
Total	**712**

The Capacity Track, provides funds to colleges and universities to expand existing educational opportunities and resources in cyber security and increase in the ability of the United States higher education enterprise to produce cyber security professionals. Examples of projects include: conducting research on the teaching and learning of cyber security, including research on materials, methods and small-scale interventions; establishing curricula recommendations for new courses, degree programs, and educational pathways with plans for wide adoption nationally; evaluating teaching and learning effectiveness of cyber security curricular programs and courses; integrating cyber security topics into computer science, information technology, engineering and other existing degree programs with plans for pervasive adoption; developing virtual laboratories to promote collaboration and resource sharing in cyber security education; strengthening partnerships between institutions of higher education, government, and relevant employment sectors leading to improved models for the integration of applied research experiences into cyber security degree programs; and evaluating the effectiveness of cyber security competitions and other outreach and retention activities.

From FY 2011 through FY 2014, the SFS program has made 117 awards totaling over $145 million and covering every region of the country.

With an emphasis on two-year colleges, the Advanced Technological Education (ATE) program focuses on the education of technicians for the high-technology fields that drive our Nation's economy, including cyber security. The program involves partnerships between academic institutions and industry to promote improvement in the education of science and engineering technicians at the undergraduate and secondary school levels. The ATE program supports curriculum development; professional development of college faculty and secondary school teachers; career pathways to two-year colleges from secondary schools and from two-year colleges to four-year institutions; and other activities. Another goal is articulation between two-year and four-year programs for K-12 prospective science, technology, engineering, and mathematics (STEM) teachers who focus on technological education.

The ATE program supports projects, centers, and targeted research on technician education. Activities may have either a national or a regional focus, but not a purely local one. A project or center is expected to communicate a realistic vision for sustainability and a plan for achievement. It is expected that at least some aspects of both centers and projects will be sustained or institutionalized past the period of award funding. Being sustainable means that a project or center has developed a product or service that the host institution, its partners, and its target audiences want continued.

Of 17 active ATE awards, four are focused on cyber security, including a national center, a resource center, and two regional centers:

- *National CyberWatch Center* (Maryland) – This center, originally established in 2005 at Prince George's Community College and re-funded as a national center in 2012, leads collaborative efforts to increase the quantity and quality of the cyber security workforce by advancing cyber security education. The center comprises over 50 two-year schools, over 50 four-year institutions in 33 states, over 30 industry partners, three government partners, six public school systems, and two non-profit organizations. It pursues curriculum development, faculty professional development, and K-12 initiatives. It is estimated that over 11,000 students have been impacted by the National CyberWatch Center's faculty development.
- *National Resource Center for Systems Security and Information Assurance (CSSIA)* (Illinois) – Originally established in 2003, this center, based at Moraine Valley Community College, seeks to support: innovative faculty development; expansion of comprehensive cyber competitions at the higher education and minority levels; development and expansive distribution of high-quality cyber security lab content; and remote virtualization content delivery and innovative virtualization lab environments. CSSIA has mentored, established, and expanded cyber security degree and certification programs at hundreds of institutions in over 30 states. In 2013 alone, 1,191 students participated in CSSIA-sponsored cyber security competitions.
- *Cyber Security Education Consortium (CSEC)* (Oklahoma) – Based at the University of Tulsa, this center is a partnership of community colleges and career and technology centers in eight states in the central U.S. CSEC has established cyber security certificate and degree programs at 49 two-year program sites in eight states, and signed over 120 articulation agreements that provide students with advanced placement, dual enrollment, or cyber security course credit at two- and four-year institutions. Since 2004, over 1,300 CSEC students have completed certificate programs in cyber security; over 800 others have received associate degrees; and over 200 others have attained bachelor's degrees in cyber security. In the 2013-14 academic year, CSEC had 2,337 security-related student enrollments.
- *CyberWatch West* (Washington) – The overarching goal of CyberWatch West is to strengthen the cyber security workforce in California and the Pacific Northwest. To accomplish this goal, CyberWatch West is concentrating on the following four major areas: (1) student activities, including meaningful internships and a cyber-defense league with weekly virtual exercises; (2) assistance in curriculum development based on recognized standards and creation of cyber security pathways from community colleges to four-year institutions; (3) a faculty development and mentor program to help infuse cyber security concepts into coursework; (4) outreach and partnership with regional

community colleges, universities, high schools, and industry to determine and assist with regional needs in cyber security education. CyberWatch West consists of 44 academic partners, plus three high-schools and 19 industry and government partners, and has an active enrollment of nearly 1,000 students, including a large minority student population.

In addition, there is an ATE large project entitled *Advanced Cyberforensics Education Consortium (ACE)* based at Daytona University (Florida), with 15 college partners in four states. ACE provides students with high-quality, hands-on educational experiences to increase marketability in the cyber security/forensics sectors of business and government. Since its establishment in January 2013, over 300 college students have completed at least one of the four core courses.

NSF has also supported several university pilots on cyber security education and secure programming. These pilots included the New Jersey Cyber Center project and New Jersey Governor's Cup; a Purdue University-led collaborative project linking student research teams with real-word projects mentored by technical directors at the National Security Agency; and an innovative competition at the University of Maryland to build secure systems.

Additionally, NSF continues to co-lead with the U.S. Department of Education the Formal Cybersecurity Education Component of the National Initiative for Cybersecurity Education (NICE). The goal of NICE is to establish an operational, sustainable and continually improving cyber security education program for the Nation to use sound cyber practices that will enhance the Nation's security. The National Institute of Standards and Technology (NIST) is leading the NICE initiative in collaboration with other federal departments and agencies, including NSF, to ensure coordination, cooperation, focus, public engagement, technology transfer and sustainability. NSF's involvement in the Formal Cybersecurity Education Component aims to bolster formal cyber security education programs encompassing kindergarten through twelfth grade, higher education and vocational programs, with a focus on the science, technology, engineering and math disciplines to provide a pipeline of skilled workers for the private sector and government.

Collaboration Across the Federal Government

Finally, it is essential to describe the National Science Foundation's close coordination and collaboration with other federal agencies pursuing cyber security research and development activities.

Cyber Security R&D Strategic Plan

As mentioned earlier, in 2011, the National Science and Technology Council (NSTC), with the cooperation of NSF, put forward a strategic plan titled *Trustworthy Cyberspace: Strategic Plan for the Federal Cybersecurity Research and Development Program*[18]. As noted in the Strategic Plan, three important principles guided its development, and NSF's approach to cyber security is aligned with these:

- The research must aim at underlying cyber security deficiencies and focus on root causes of vulnerabilities – that is, we need to understand and address the causes of cyber security problems as opposed to just treating their symptoms.
- The Strategic Plan must channel expertise and resources from a wide range of disciplines and sectors. Cyber security is a multi-dimensional challenge, involving both the strength of security technologies and variability of human behavior. Therefore, solutions will depend not only on

---

[18] http://www.whitehouse.gov/sites/default/files/microsites/ostp/fed_cybersecurity_rd_strategic_plan_2011.pdf

51

expertie in mathematics, computer science, and electrical engineering, but also in biology, economics, and other social and behavioral sciences.

- Cyber security principles must be enduring, allowing us to stay secure despite changes in technologies and in the threat environment. Whether we use desktop computers, tablets, mobile phones, control systems, Internet-enabled household appliances, or other cyberspace-enabled devices yet to be invented, we must be able to maintain and fulfill our trust requirements to ensure our continued security and safety.

The Plan specifies four strategic thrusts to organize activities and drive progress in cyber security R&D across the federal government:

- Inducing Change – Utilizing game-changing themes to direct efforts towards understanding the underlying root causes of known current threats with the goal of disrupting the status quo with radically different approaches to improve the security of the critical cyber systems and infrastructure that serve society.
- Developing Scientific Foundations – Developing an organized, cohesive scientific foundation to the body of knowledge that informs the field of cyber security through adoption of a systematic, rigorous, and disciplined scientific approach. Promotes the discovery of laws, hypothesis testing, repeatable experimental designs, standardized data-gathering methods, metrics, common terminology, and critical analysis that engenders reproducible results and rationally based conclusions.
- Maximizing Research Impact – Catalyzing integration across the game-changing R&D themes, cooperation between governmental and private-sector communities, collaboration across international borders, and strengthened linkages to other national priorities, such as health IT and Smart Grid.
- Accelerating Transition to Practice – Focusing efforts to ensure adoption and implementation of the powerful new technologies and strategies that emerge from the research themes, and the activities to build a scientific foundation so as to create measurable improvements in the cyber security landscape.

Finally, rather than focusing on specific technical problems and solutions, the Strategic Plan articulates desired end-states and capabilities, thereby inviting a diversity of approaches and encouraging innovation across disciplines and sectors. The research themes that are prioritized in the Plan and worthy of further inquiry include:

- The science of cyber security will develop the underlying fundamental principles that allow for the adoption of a more scientific approach to building, maintaining, and using trustworthy systems.
- The designed-in security theme focuses on developing capabilities to design and evolve high-assurance systems resistant to cyber-attacks, whose assurance properties can be verified. Such development capabilities offer the path to dramatic increases in the security and safety of software systems.
- Moving target defense research aspires to elude attackers through diverse, shifting, and increasingly complex cyber techniques and mechanisms.
- The tailored trustworthy spaces theme supports research into varying trustworthy space policies and services that are context specific with the aim to create flexible, distributed trust environments.

- The cyber economic incentives theme focuses on research at the interstices of the economic and computer sciences to achieve secure practices through market mechanisms and behavioral incentives.

Coordination Across the Government

Beyond the Strategic Plan, NSF coordinates its cyber security research and planning activities with other federal agencies, including the Departments of Defense (DoD) and Homeland Security (DHS) and the agencies of the Intelligence Community, through various "mission-bridging" activities:

- NSF plays a leadership role in the interagency Networking and Information Technology Research and Development (NITRD) Program. The National Science and Technology Council's NITRD Subcommittee, of which I am co-chair, has played a prominent role in the coordination of the federal government's cyber security research investments.
- In January 2008, President Bush initiated the Comprehensive National Cyber Security Initiative (CNCI)[19]. The current Administration supports and has continued efforts on this initiative. One of the goals of the CNCI is to develop "leap-ahead" technologies that would achieve orders-of-magnitude improvements in cyber security.
- Based on this directive, a NITRD Senior Steering Group (SSG) for Cyber Security and Information Assurance R&D (CSIA R&D)[20] was established to provide a responsive and robust conduit for cyber security R&D information across the policy, fiscal, and research levels of the government. The SSG is composed of senior representatives of agencies with national cyber security leadership positions, including: DoD, Office of the Director of National Intelligence (ODNI), DHS, NSA, NSF, NIST, Office of Science and Technology Policy, and Office of Management and Budget. A principal responsibility of the SSG is to define, coordinate, and recommend strategic federal R&D objectives in cyber security, and to communicate research needs and proposed budget priorities to policy makers and budget officials. One of CISE's Division Directors is the co-chair of this group.
- The NITRD Cyber Security and Information Assurance Interagency Working Group (CSIA IWG)[21] coordinates cyber security and information assurance research and development across the member agencies, including DoD, the Department of Energy and the National Security Agency, which focus on research and development to prevent, resist, detect, respond to, and/or recover from actions that compromise or threaten to compromise the availability, integrity, or confidentiality of computer- and network-based systems.
- To facilitate cross conversation between classified and unclassified programs in the federal government, a coordinating group called Special Cyber Operations Research and Engineering (SCORE) was established. SCORE, which includes members from the CSIA R&D SSG and IWG, is intended to work in parallel to the CSIA R&D IWG. NSF research is reported in this forum.
- Under the auspices of the NITRD program and the CSIA SSG and IWG, NSF and the other member agencies have co-funded and co-sponsored several workshops, including in FY 2014:

---

[19] http://www.nitrd.gov/subcommittee/csiacyberlink.html

[20] https://www.nitrd.gov/nitrdgroups/index.php?title=Cyber_Security_Information_Assurance_Research_and_Development_Senior_Steering_Group_%28CSIA_R%26D_SSG%29

[21] https://www.nitrd.gov/nitrdgroups/index.php?title=Cyber_Security_and_Information_Assurance_Interagency_Working_Group_(CSIA_IWG)

- A "Science of Cyber Security" workshop that considered specific foundational problems (e.g., metrics, fundamental results, evidence-based research, and protection of critical infrastructure); and
- A "Cyber Security 2025" workshop that sought to catalyze a community-wide discussion to review progress relative to the federal strategic plan and to envision long-term research agendas for the field.

- In February 2014, NSF convened a workshop with participation from across the federal government as well as academe and the private sector to generate actionable ideas that could potentially be pursued or adopted by cyber security researchers, policymakers, or practitioners to advance cyber security. The recommendations that emerged from the workshop are grouped into three categories – technology, policy, and leadership – and are described in detail in the final report[22].
- Through NITRD, NSF and the DHS Science and Technology Directorate have worked together to identify and co-fund emerging security technologies that will transition into operational use in both the private sector and government. The first example of this collaboration is the ShellOS project at the University of North Carolina at Chapel Hill[23], which identifies malware in email attachments more rapidly and accurately than commercial products, and stops such malware attacks before users can download the infected attachments.

An Increasing Emphasis on Privacy R&D

Through the CSIA R&D SSG, NSF is supporting the development of a National Privacy Research Strategy (NPRS) that will establish objectives and prioritization guidance for federally-funded privacy research, provide a framework for coordinating R&D in privacy-enhancing technologies, and encourage multi-disciplinary research that recognizes the responsibilities of the government and needs of society, and that enhances opportunities for innovation in the digital realm. As part of this effort, the CSIA R&D SSG published a Request for Information in September 2014[24]. On the basis of this input[25], the CSIA R&D SSG is convening a cross-sector workshop in February 2015 to surface key privacy perspectives, needs, and challenges that should be considered in forming a privacy research strategy; to gain a better understanding of what objectives should guide federal privacy research; and to examine prospective research themes that might be used to organize and prioritize federal research in privacy. The workshop, which will span government, commercial, individual, and societal perspectives, aims to decompose privacy into areas where goals for privacy research could be established; create a framework that links privacy research objectives into a coherent picture; and formulate research objectives in ways that invite a variety of contributions and approaches from many disciplines. The National Privacy Research Strategy follows a review by the National Coordination Office (NCO) on privacy research activities pursued by agencies in NITRD that sought to understand what research is taking place and to begin exploring a multi-agency research agenda in the foundations of privacy[26].

Conclusions

My testimony today has emphasized that the pace and scope of today's cyber threats pose grand challenges to our national critical infrastructure, and that NSF has been making, and continues to make,

---

[22] http://www.nsf.gov/cise/news/CybersecurityIdeasLab_July2014.pdf
[23] https://www.usenix.org/legacy/event/sec11/tech/full_papers/Snow.pdf
[24] https://federalregister.gov/a/2014-22239
[25] https://www.nitrd.gov/cybersecurity/nationalprivacyresearchstrategy.aspx
[26] https://www.nitrd.gov/Pubs/Report_on_Privacy_Research_within_NITRD.pdf

significant investments across multiple directorates in foundational and multi-disciplinary cyber security research, resulting in important advances over the years as well as identifying fundamentally new research directions and creating opportunities for the future. Indeed, our Nation needs to continue to invest in long-term, fundamental and game-changing research if our cyber systems are to remain trustworthy in the future. I have also described how NSF's interdisciplinary research and education portfolios are contributing to a next-generation workforce that is increasingly cyber-aware, armed with the knowledge that it needs to protect against cyber attacks. I have discussed how NSF partners with industry and other government agencies to address cyber threats and to advance cyber security R&D. I appreciate the opportunity to have this dialogue with members of this Subcommittee on these very important topics. With robust sustained support for cyber security research and development in both the executive and legislative branches, there is a unique opportunity to protect our national security and enhance our economic prosperity for decades to come. This concludes my remarks. I would be happy to answer any questions at this time.

Biographical Sketch

JAMES F. KUROSE

James F. Kurose is the National Science Foundation Assistant Director for the Computer and Information Science and Engineering (CISE) Directorate. Prior to joining NSF, he was a Distinguished Professor in the School of Computer Science at the University of Massachusetts Amherst, where he led research projects on computer network protocols and architecture, network measurement, sensor networks, multimedia communication, and modeling and performance evaluation. Dr. Kurose also currently serves as co-chair of the Networking and Information Technology Research and Development (NITRD) Subcommittee of the National Science and Technology Council (NSTC) Committee on Technology, providing overall coordination for the IT R&D activities of 18 federal government agencies and offices.

At NSF, Dr. Kurose guides the CISE directorate in its mission to advance the Nation's leadership in computer and information science and engineering through its support for fundamental and transformative research, as well as the development and use of cyberinfrastructure across the science and engineering enterprise. These activities are critical to ensuring economic competitiveness and achieving national priorities. With a budget of nearly $900 million, CISE supports ambitious long-term research and innovation, advanced cyberinfrastructure to enable and accelerate discovery and innovation across all disciplines, broad interdisciplinary collaborations, and education and training of the next generation of computer scientists and information technology professionals with skills essential to success in the increasingly competitive, global market.

Over the last three decades at the University of Massachusetts Amherst, Dr. Kurose served in a number of administrative roles including chair of the Department of Computer Science, interim dean and executive associate dean of the College of Natural Sciences, and senior faculty advisor to the Vice Chancellor for Research and Engagement. He has been a visiting scientist at IBM Research, INRIA, Institut EURECOM, the University of Paris, the Laboratory for Information, Network and Communication Sciences, and Technicolor Research Labs. He helped found and lead the Commonwealth Information Technology Initiative and the Massachusetts Green High Performance Computing Center.

He has served as editor-in-chief of the Institute of Electrical and Electronics Engineers (IEEE) *Transactions on Communications* and was the founding editor-in-chief of the *IEEE/ACM* (Association for Computing Machinery) *Transactions on Networking.* With Keith Ross, he coauthored the textbook, *Computer Networking: A Top-Down Approach,* which is in its sixth edition.

Dr. Kurose has received recognition for his research, including the IEEE Infocom Achievement Award and the ACM Sigcomm Test of Time award. He has also been recognized for his educational activities, receiving the IEEE/CS Taylor Booth Education medal and the Massachusetts Telecommunication Council Workforce Development Leader of the Year award.

Dr. Kurose has served on a variety of advisory boards, including on the CISE advisory committee and the Board of Directors for the Computing Research Association.

Dr. Kurose holds a Bachelor of Arts degree in physics from Wesleyan University, and a Master of Science and a Ph.D. in computer science from Columbia University. He is a fellow of the IEEE and ACM.

Chairwoman COMSTOCK. All right. Thank you, Doctor.
And now we now recognize Dr. Romine for his testimony.

**TESTIMONY OF DR. CHARLES H. ROMINE, DIRECTOR,
INFORMATION TECHNOLOGY LABORATORY,
NATIONAL INSTITUTE OF STANDARDS AND TECHNOLOGY**

Dr. ROMINE. Chairwoman Comstock, Chairman Smith, Mr. Lipinski, and Members of the Subcommittee, I am Dr. Charles Romine, Director of the Information Technology Laboratory at NIST, and thank you for the opportunity to discuss our role in cybersecurity.

In the area of cybersecurity, NIST has worked with federal agencies, industry, and academia since 1972. Our role—to research, develop, and deploy information security standards and technology to protect information systems against threats to the confidentiality, integrity, and availability of information and services—was strengthened through the Computer Security Act of 1987, broadened through the Federal Information Security Management Act of 2002, and recently reaffirmed in the Federal Information Security Modernization Act of 2014. The Cybersecurity Enhancement Act of 2014 also authorizes NIST to facilitate and support the development of voluntary, industry-led cybersecurity standards and best practices for critical infrastructure.

NIST accomplishes its mission in cybersecurity through collaborative partnerships. The resulting NIST special publications and interagency reports provide operational and technical security guidelines for federal agencies and cover a broad range of topics such as electronic authentication, intrusion detection, access control, and malware.

NIST maintains the National Vulnerability Database, or NVD, a repository of standards-based vulnerability management reference data, which enables security automation capabilities for all organizations. The payment card industry uses the NVD vulnerability metrics to discern the IT vulnerability in point-of-sale devices and determine acceptable risk.

NIST researchers develop and standardize cryptographic mechanisms used worldwide to protect information. The NIST algorithms and guidelines are developed in a transparent and inclusive process leveraging cryptographic expertise around the world. The results are standard, interoperable, cryptographic mechanisms that can be used by all.

Recently, NIST initiated a research program on usability of cybersecurity focused on password policies, user perceptions of cybersecurity risk, and privacy. This will enhance cybersecurity through increased attention to user interactions with cybersecurity technologies.

The impacts of NIST's cybersecurity activities extend beyond providing the means to protect federal IT systems. They provide the cybersecurity foundations for the public trust that is essential to realizing the national and global economic, productivity, and innovation potential of electronic business. Many organizations voluntarily follow NIST standards and guidelines reflecting their worldwide acceptance.

NIST also houses the National Program Office of the National Strategy for Trusted Identities in Cyberspace, or NSTIC. The

NSTIC initiative aims to address one of the most commonly exploited vectors of attack in cyberspace, the inadequacy of passwords for authentication. The 2013 data breach investigations report noted that in 2012 76 percent of network intrusions exploited weak or stolen credentials. NSTIC is addressing this issue by collaborating with the private sector, including funding 13 pilots, to catalyze a marketplace of better identity and authentication systems.

Another critical component of NIST cybersecurity work is the National Cybersecurity Center of Excellence, or NCCoE, a partnership between NIST, the State of Maryland, Montgomery County, and the private sector. NCCoE is accelerating the adoption of applied, standards-based solutions to cybersecurity challenges. The NCCOE is now supported by the nation's first federally funded research and development center dedicated to cybersecurity.

Through NCCoE, NIST works directly with businesses across various industry sectors on applied solutions to cybersecurity challenges with current activities addressing the healthcare, financial services, and energy sectors.

Almost one year ago NIST issued the Framework for Improving Critical Infrastructure Cybersecurity in response to Executive Order 13636. The framework, created through collaboration between industry and government, consists of standards, guidelines, and practices to promote the protection of critical infrastructure. The framework is being implemented by industry and adopted by infrastructure sectors to reduce cyber risks to our critical infrastructure.

As the cyber threats and technology environments evolve, the cybersecurity workforce must continue to adapt so as to continuously improve cybersecurity, including in our nation's critical infrastructure. In 2010, the National Initiative for Cybersecurity Education was established to enhance the overall cybersecurity posture of the United States by accelerating the availability of educational, training, and workforce development resources designed to improve the cybersecurity behavior, skills, and knowledge of every segment of the population.

As the lead agency for this initiative, NIST works with more than 20 federal departments and agencies, industry, and academia to raise national awareness about risks in cyberspace, broaden the pool of individuals prepared to enter the cybersecurity profession, and cultivate a globally competitive cybersecurity workforce.

NIST recognizes our essential role in helping industry, consumers, and government to counter cyber threats. We are extremely proud of our role in establishing and improving the comprehensive set of cybersecurity technical solutions, standards, guidelines, and best practices, and the robust collaborations with our federal government partners, private sector collaborators, and international colleagues.

Thank you for the opportunity to testify today on NIST's work in cybersecurity. I would be happy to answer any questions that you may have.

[The prepared statement of Dr. Romine follows:]

Testimony of

Charles H. Romine
Director
Information Technology Laboratory
National Institute of Standards and Technology
United States Department of Commerce

United States House of Representatives

Committee on Science, Space and Technology

Subcommittee on Research and Technology

"The Expanding Cyber Threat"

January 27, 2015

Introduction

Chairwoman Comstock, Ranking Member and Members of the Subcommittee, I am Dr. Charles Romine, the Director of the Information Technology Laboratory (ITL) at the Department of Commerce's National Institute of Standards and Technology (NIST). Thank you for the opportunity to appear before you today to discuss our role in cybersecurity.

The Role of NIST in Cybersecurity

With programs focused on national priorities from the Smart Grid and electronic health records to forensics, atomic clocks, advanced nanomaterials, and computer chips and more, NIST's overall mission is to promote U.S. innovation and industrial competitiveness by advancing measurement science, standards, and technology in ways that enhance economic security and improve our quality of life.

In the area of cybersecurity, NIST has worked with Federal agencies, industry, and academia since 1972, starting with the development of the Data Encryption Standard, when the potential commercial benefit of this technology became clear. Our role, to research, develop and deploy information security standards and technology to protect the Federal government's information systems against threats to the confidentiality, integrity and availability of information and services, was strengthened through the Computer Security Act of 1987 (Public Law 100-235), broadened through the Federal Information Security Management Act of 2002 (FISMA; 44 U.S.C. § 3541[1]) and recently reaffirmed in the Federal Information Security Modernization Act of 2014 (Public Law 113-283). In addition, the Cybersecurity Enhancement Act of 2014 (Public Law 113-274) authorizes NIST to facilitate and support the development of voluntary, industry-led cybersecurity standards and best practices for critical infrastructure.

NIST accomplishes its mission in cybersecurity through collaborative partnerships with our customers and stakeholders in industry, government, academia, standards bodies, consortia and international partners.

We employ collaborative partnerships with our customers and stakeholders to take advantage of their technical and operational insights and to leverage the resources of a global community. These collaborative efforts and our private sector collaborations in particular, are constantly being expanded by new initiatives, including in recent years through the National Strategy for Trusted Identities in Cyberspace (NSTIC), the National Cybersecurity Center of Excellence (NCCoE), in implementation of Executive Order 13636, "Improving Critical Infrastructure Cybersecurity," and the National Initiative for Cybersecurity Education (NICE).

---

[1] FISMA was enacted as Title III of the E-Government Act of 2002 (Public Law 107-347; 116 Stat. 2899).

NIST Cybersecurity Research, Standards and Guidelines

The NIST Special Publications and Interagency Reports provide management, operational, and technical security guidelines for Federal agency information systems, and cover a broad range of topics such as Basic Input/Output System (BIOS) management and measurement, key management and derivation, media sanitization, electronic authentication, security automation, Bluetooth and wireless protocols, incident handling and intrusion detection, malware, cloud computing, public key infrastructure, risk assessments, supply chain risk management, authentication, access control, security automation and continuous monitoring.

Beyond these documents - which are peer-reviewed throughout industry, government, and academia - NIST conducts workshops, awareness briefings, and outreach to ensure comprehension of standards and guidelines, to share ongoing and planned activities, and to aid in scoping guidelines in a collaborative, open, and transparent manner.

In addition, NIST maintains the National Vulnerability Database (NVD), a repository of standards-based vulnerability management reference data. The NVD makes available information on vulnerabilities, impact measurements, detection techniques, and remediation assistance. It provides reference data that enable government, industry and international security automation capabilities. The NVD also plays a role in the efforts of the Payment Card Industry (PCI) to identify and mitigate vulnerabilities. The PCI uses the NVD vulnerability metrics to discern the IT vulnerability in point-of-sale devices and determine what risks are unacceptable for that industry.

NIST researchers develop and standardize cryptographic mechanisms that are used throughout the world to protect information at rest and in transit. These mechanisms provide security services, such as confidentiality, integrity, authentication, non-repudiation and digital signatures, to protect sensitive information. The NIST algorithms and associated cryptographic guidelines are developed in a transparent and inclusive process, leveraging cryptographic expertise around the world. The results are in standard, interoperable cryptographic mechanisms that can be used by all industries.

NIST has a complementary program, in coordination with the Government of Canada, to certify independent commercial calibration laboratories to test commercially available IT cryptographic modules, to ensure that they have implemented the NIST cryptographic standards and guidelines correctly. These testing laboratories exist around the globe and test hundreds of individual cryptographic modules yearly.

Recently, NIST initiated a research program in usability of cybersecurity, focused on passwords and password policies; user perceptions of cybersecurity risk and privacy concerns; and privacy in general. The concept of "usability" refers generally to "the effectiveness, efficiency, and satisfaction with which the intended users can achieve

61

their tasks in the intended context of product use."[2] NIST's hope is that this usability research will lead to standards and guidelines for improving cybersecurity through increased attention to user interactions with security technologies.

NIST Engagement with Industry

It is important to note that the impact of NIST's activities under FISMA extend beyond providing the means to protect Federal IT systems. They provide the cybersecurity foundations for the public trust that is essential to our realization of the national and global productivity and innovation potential of electronic business and its attendant economic benefits. Many organizations voluntarily follow NIST standards and guidelines, reflecting their wide acceptance throughout the world.

Beyond NIST's responsibilities under FISMA, under the provisions of the National Technology Transfer and Advancement Act (PL 104-113) and related OMB Circular A-119, NIST is tasked with the key role of encouraging and coordinating Federal agency use of voluntary consensus standards and participation in the development of relevant standards, as well as promoting coordination between the public and private sectors in the development of standards and in conformity assessment activities. NIST works with other agencies, such as the Department of State, to coordinate standards issues and priorities with the private sector through consensus standards organizations such as the American National Standards Institute (ANSI), the International Organization for Standardization (ISO), the Institute of Electrical and Electronics Engineers (IEEE), the Internet Engineering Task Force (IETF), and the International Telecommunications Union (ITU).

Partnership with industry to develop, maintain, and implement voluntary consensus standards related to cybersecurity best ensures the interoperability, security and resiliency of the global infrastructure needed to make us all more secure. It also allows this infrastructure to evolve in a way that embraces both security and innovation -- allowing a market to flourish to create new types of secure products for the benefit of all Americans.

NIST works extensively in smart card standards, guidelines and best practices. NIST developed the standard for the US Government Personal Identity Verification (PIV) Card, and actively works with the ANSI and the ISO on global cybersecurity standards for use in smart cards, smart card cryptography and the standards for the international integrated circuit card. [ANSI 504; ISO 7816 and ISO 24727]

NIST also conducts cybersecurity research and development in forward looking technology areas, such as security for federal mobile environments and techniques for measuring and managing security. These efforts focus on improving the trustworthiness of IT components such as claimed identities, data, hardware, and software for networks and devices. Additional research areas include developing approaches to balancing safety, security, and reliability in the nation's information and

---

[2] International Organization for Standardization (ISO), ISO 9241-11 (1998): "Ergonomic requirements for office work with visual display terminals (VDTs) -- Guidance on usability."

communications technology supply chain; enabling mobile device and application security; securing the nation's cyber-physical systems and public safety networks; enabling continuous security monitoring; providing advanced security measurements and testing; investigating security analytics and big data; developing standards, modeling, and measurements to achieve end-to-end security over heterogeneous, multi-domain networks; and investigating technologies for detection of anomalous behavior and quarantines.

In addition, further development of cybersecurity standards will be needed to improve the security and resiliency of critical U.S. information and communication infrastructure. The availability of cybersecurity standards and associated conformity assessment schemes is essential in these efforts, which NIST supports to help enhance the deployment of sound security solutions and builds trust among those creating and those using the solutions throughout the country.

National Strategy for Trusted Identities in Cyberspace

NIST also houses the National Program Office established to lead implementation of the National Strategy for Trusted Identities in Cyberspace (NSTIC). NSTIC is an initiative that aims to address one of the most commonly exploited vectors of attack in cyberspace: the inadequacy of passwords for authentication.

The 2013 Data Breach Investigations Report noted that in 2012, 76% of network intrusions exploited weak or stolen credentials. In line with the results of this report, Target has revealed that the compromised credential of one of its business partners was the vector used to access its network.

NSTIC aims to address this issue by collaborating with the private sector to catalyze a marketplace of better identity and authentication solutions – an "Identity Ecosystem" that raises the level of trust associated with the identities of individuals, organizations, networks, services, and devices online. NIST has funded 13 pilots to help jumpstart the marketplace and test new approaches to overcome barriers, such as usability, privacy and interoperability, which have hindered market acceptance and wider use of stronger authentication technologies.

NSTIC exemplifies NIST's robust collaboration with industry, in large part, because the initiative calls on the private sector to play a lead role in its implementation. NIST has partnered with a privately led Identity Ecosystem Steering Group (IDESG) to craft better standards and tools to improve authentication online.

National Cybersecurity Center of Excellence

In 2012, the National Cybersecurity Center of Excellence (NCCoE) was formed as a partnership between NIST, the State of Maryland, and Montgomery County to accelerate the adoption of security technologies that are based on standards and best practices. Recently, NIST established the Nation's first Federally Funded Research and Development Center (FFRDC) dedicated to cybersecurity to support the NCCoE. The center is a vehicle for NIST to work directly with businesses across various industry sectors on applied solutions to cybersecurity challenges. Today the NCCoE has programs working with the healthcare, financial services, and energy sectors in addition to addressing challenges that cut across sectors including: mobile device security, software asset management, cloud security, and identity management.

Today NIST's NCCoE is working with government and industry partners on a number of projects including the Security Exchange of Electronic Health Information. This project focuses on securely exchanging information through the use of mobile devices. NIST plans to publish a practice guide for this project in the near future which will provide members of the technology community the materials list, configuration settings and other information they need to replicate this standards-based security solution.

Cybersecurity Framework

Almost one year ago, NIST issued the Framework for Improving Critical Infrastructure Cybersecurity (Framework) in accordance with Section 7 of Executive Order 13636, "Improving Critical Infrastructure Cybersecurity." The Framework, created through collaboration between industry and government, consists of standards, guidelines, and practices to promote the protection of critical infrastructure. The prioritized, flexible, repeatable, and cost-effective approach of the Framework helps owners and operators of critical infrastructure to manage cybersecurity-related risk.

Since the release of the Framework, NIST has strengthened its collaborations with critical infrastructure owners and operators, industry leaders, government partners, and other stakeholders to raise awareness about the Framework, encourage use by organizations across and supporting the critical infrastructure, and develop implementation guides and resources. The Framework continues to be voluntarily implemented by industry and adopted by infrastructure sectors, and this is contributing to reducing cyber risks to our Nation's critical infrastructure.

National Initiative for Cybersecurity Education

As the cybersecurity threat and technology environment evolves, the cybersecurity workforce must continue to adapt to design, develop, implement, maintain and continuously improve cybersecurity, including in our Nation's critical infrastructure.

In 2010, the National Initiative for Cybersecurity Education (NICE) was established to enhance the overall cybersecurity posture of the United States by accelerating the availability of educational, training, and workforce development resources designed to improve the cybersecurity behavior, skills, and knowledge of every segment of the population. As the lead agency for this initiative, NIST works with more than 20 Federal departments and agencies, as well as with industry and academia, to raise national awareness about risks in cyberspace, broaden the pool of individuals prepared to enter the cybersecurity profession, and cultivate a globally competitive cybersecurity workforce.

NICE has also aligned with the President's Job-Driven Training Initiative to increase the number of individuals who complete high-quality cybersecurity training and education programs and attain the skills most needed to provide a pipeline of skilled workers for industry and government.

Additional Research Areas

NIST performs research and development in related technologies, such as the usability of systems including electronic health records, voting machines, biometrics and software interfaces. NIST is performing basic research on the mathematical foundations needed to determine the security of information systems. In the areas of digital forensics, NIST is enabling improvements in forensic analysis through the National Software Reference Library and computer forensics tool testing. Software assurance metrics, tools, and evaluations developed at NIST are being implemented by industry to help strengthen software against hackers. NIST responds to government and market requirements for biometric standards by collaborating with other Federal agencies, academia, and industry partners to develop and implement biometrics evaluations, enable usability, and develop standards (fingerprint, face, iris, voice/speaker, and multimodal biometrics). NIST plays a central role in defining and advancing standards, and collaborating with customers and stakeholders to identify and reach consensus on cloud computing standards.

Conclusion

We at NIST recognize that we have an essential role to play in helping industry, consumers and government to counter cyber threats. Our broader work in the areas of information security, trusted networks, and software quality is applicable to a wide variety of users, from small and medium enterprises to large private and public organizations, including Federal government agencies and companies involved with critical infrastructure.

We are extremely proud of our role in establishing and improving the comprehensive set of cybersecurity technical solutions, standards, guidelines, and best practices and the robust collaborations with our Federal government partners, private sector collaborators, and international colleagues.

Thank you for the opportunity to testify today on NIST's work in cybersecurity. I would be happy to answer any questions you may have.

Charles H. Romine

Charles Romine is Director of the Information Technology Laboratory (ITL). ITL, one of seven research Laboratories within the National Institute of Standards and Technology (NIST), has an annual budget of $150 million, more than 350 employees, and about 160 guest researchers from industry, universities, and foreign laboratories.

Dr. Romine oversees a research program designed to promote U.S. innovation and industrial competitiveness by developing and disseminating standards, measurements, and testing for interoperability, security, usability, and reliability of information systems, including cybersecurity standards and guidelines for Federal agencies and U.S. industry, supporting these and measurement science at NIST through fundamental and applied research in computer science, mathematics, and statistics. Through its efforts, ITL supports NIST's mission, to promote U.S. innovation and industrial competitiveness by advancing measurement science, standards, and technology in ways that enhance economic security and improve our quality of life.

Within NIST's traditional role as the overseer of the National Measurement System, ITL is conducting research addressing measurement challenges in information technology as well as issues of information and software quality, integrity, and usability. ITL is also charged with leading the Nation in using existing and emerging IT to help meet national priorities, including developing cybersecurity standards, guidelines, and associated methods and techniques, cloud computing, electronic voting, smart grid, homeland security applications, and health information technology.

Education:

Ph.D. in Applied Mathematics from the University of Virginia

B.A. in Mathematics from the University of Virginia.

Chairwoman COMSTOCK. Thank you, Doctor.
And now I recognize Dr. Fischer for his testimony.

**TESTIMONY OF DR. ERIC A. FISCHER,
SENIOR SPECIALIST IN SCIENCE AND TECHNOLOGY,
CONGRESSIONAL RESEARCH SERVICE**

Dr. FISCHER. Good afternoon, Chairwoman Comstock, Chairman Smith, Ranking Member Lipinski, and distinguished Members of the Subcommittee. On behalf of the Congressional Research Service, thank you for the opportunity to testify today.

I will try to put what you have heard from previous witnesses in context with respect to both long-term challenges and near-term needs in cybersecurity and the federal role in addressing them.

The technologies that process and communicate information have become ubiquitous and are increasingly integral to almost every facet of modern life. These technologies and the information they manage are collectively known as a cyberspace, which may well be the most rapidly evolving technology space in human history. This growth refers not only to how big cyberspace is but also to what it is. Social media, mobile devices, cloud computing, big data, and the internet of things— these are all recent developments and all are increasingly important facets of cyberspace. It is difficult to predict how cyberspace will continue to evolve but it is probably safe to expect the evolution to continue for many years.

That is not to say that all of cyberspace has changed. Basic aspects of how the internet works are decades old, and obsolete hardware, software, and practices may persist for many years. All of this makes the cyberspace environment a daunting challenge for cybersecurity. Three other major challenges relate to design, incentives, and consensus. Building security into the design of cyberspace has proven to be difficult. The incentive structure within cyberspace does not particularly favor cybersecurity, and significant barriers persist for developing consensus on what cybersecurity to involves and how to implement it effectively.

No matter how important such challenges are, they do not diminish the need to secure cyberspace in the short-term. That includes reducing risk by removing threats, hardening vulnerabilities, and taking steps to lessen the impacts of cyber attacks. It also includes addressing needs such as reducing barriers to information-sharing, building a capable cybersecurity workforce, and fighting cybercrime.

Federal agencies play significant roles in addressing those near-term needs and meeting the long-term challenges. Under the Federal Information Security Management Act, known as FISMA, all federal agencies are responsible for securing their own systems. Private-sector contractors acting on behalf of federal agencies must also meet FISMA requirements. In Fiscal Year 2013, federal agencies spent $10.3 billion on those activities, about 14 percent of agency information-technology budgets. federal agencies also have responsibilities for other cybersecurity functions. Research and development, along with education, are the two probably most focused on addressing long-term challenges. Others, such as technical standards and support, law enforcement, and regulation, focus more on meeting immediate needs.

You have already heard about NIST and NSF. Among other agencies, the Department of Energy supports cybersecurity efforts in the energy sector. Several of its 17 National Laboratories also engage in cybersecurity R&D and education. The Department of Defense, in addition to military operations, also engages in cybersecurity R&D and education. Altogether, DOD agencies account for more than 60 percent of reported federal funding for cybersecurity R&D.

The Department of Homeland Security fulfills several cybersecurity functions. In the Science and Technology Directorate, the Cybersecurity Division focuses on developing and delivering new cybersecurity technologies and other tools. The Department spent $75 million on cybersecurity R&D in 2013, more than DOE and NIST but also less than NSF and much less than DOD.

Another department responsibility is coordinating the operational security of federal systems under FISMA. The department also plays a significant role in law enforcement but perhaps is best known for coordinating federal efforts to improve the security of critical infrastructure, most of which is controlled by the private sector.

Most private-sector department activities are voluntary, but the department also has some regulatory authority over the transportation and chemical sectors. Several other agencies also have regulatory responsibilities relating to cybersecurity in the 16 recognized critical infrastructure sectors.

The role of federal regulation in cybersecurity has been a significant source of controversy, along with how to remove barriers to information-sharing while protecting proprietary and personal information, and the proper roles of different federal agencies in various cybersecurity activities.

That concludes my testimony. Once again, thank you for asking me to appear before you today.

[The prepared statement of Dr. Fischer follows:]

Statement of Eric A. Fischer
Senior Specialist in Science and Technology
Congressional Research Service

Before

Subcommittee on Research and Technology
Committee on Science, Space, and Technology
U.S. House of Representatives

January 27, 2015

on

"The Expanding Cyber Threat"

Chairwoman Comstock, Ranking Member Johnson, and distinguished Members of the Subcommittee:

Thank you for the opportunity to discuss issues related to cybersecurity with you today. In my testimony, I will provide an overview of federal cybersecurity activities related to science and technology (S&T). As you requested, I will also address long-term challenges the federal government faces related to cybersecurity, differing views about the federal role in cybersecurity, and how the *Cybersecurity Enhancement Act of 2014* (P.L. 113-274) affects existing cybersecurity efforts.

The information technology (IT) industry has evolved greatly over the last half century. Continued, exponential progress in processing power and memory capacity has made IT hardware not only faster, but also smaller, lighter, cheaper, and easier to use.

The original IT industry has also increasingly converged with the communications industry into what is commonly called information and communications technology (ICT). This technology is ubiquitous and increasingly integral to almost every facet of modern society. ICT devices and components are generally interdependent, and disruption of one may affect many others.

Over the past several years, experts and policy makers have expressed increasing concerns about protecting ICT systems from *cyberattacks*—deliberate, unauthorized attempts to access the systems, usually with the goal of theft, disruption, damage, or other unlawful actions. Many experts expect the number and severity of cyberattacks to increase over the next several years.

The act of protecting ICT systems and their contents has come to be known as *cybersecurity*. A broad and arguably somewhat fuzzy concept, cybersecurity can be a useful umbrella term but tends to defy precise consensus definition. Generally speaking, it refers to various measures intended to protect ICT components and content—collectively known as *cyberspace*[1]—from cyberattacks. Cyberspace includes computers and other ICT devices, related hardware and software, the networks that connect them, and the information they contain and communicate. Cybersecurity can also refer to the state or quality of being protected from such attacks, or to the broad field of endeavor aimed at implementing and improving protection.

Cybersecurity is also sometimes conflated in public discussion with other concepts such as privacy, information sharing, intelligence gathering, and surveillance. Privacy is associated with the ability of an individual person to control access by others to information about that person. Thus, good cybersecurity can help protect privacy in an electronic environment, but information that is shared to assist in cybersecurity efforts might sometimes contain personal data that at least some observers would regard as private. Cybersecurity can be a means of protecting against undesired surveillance of and gathering of intelligence from an information system. However, when aimed at potential sources of cyberattacks, such surveillance and information-gathering activities can also be useful to help effect cybersecurity. In addition, surveillance in the form of monitoring of information flow within a system can be an important component of cybersecurity.[2]

Overview of Federal Agency Cybersecurity Activities

The federal role in cybersecurity is complex. It involves both securing federal systems and assisting in the protection of nonfederal systems. No single overarching framework legislation is in place, but many enacted statutes address various aspects of cybersecurity. More than 50 federal statutes address various aspects of cybersecurity.[3] Under the Federal Information Security Management Act (FISMA, 44 U.S.C. Chapter 35, Subchapter II, as amended by P.L. 113-256), all federal agencies have cybersecurity responsibilities relating to their own systems. Responsibility for other cybersecurity functions is distributed among several federal agencies under FISMA and other statutes. Those functions[4] relating to S&T include

- performing and supporting *research and development* (R&D);

- developing *technical standards*;

- providing *technical support* in cybersecurity to government and private-sector entities, especially critical infrastructure (CI) entities;

---

[1] The term *cyberspace* usually refers to the worldwide collection of connected ICT components, the information that is stored in and flows through those components, and the ways that information is structured and processed (CRS Report RL32777, *Creating a National Framework for Cybersecurity: An Analysis of Issues and Options*, by Eric A. Fischer).

[2] See, for example, Department of Homeland Security, "Continuous Diagnostics and Mitigation (CDM)," June 24, 2014, http://www.dhs.gov/cdm.

[3] CRS Report R42114, *Federal Laws Relating to Cybersecurity: Overview of Major Issues, Current Laws, and Proposed Legislation,* by Eric A. Fischer.

[4] These functions are not necessarily mutually exclusive. For example, development of technical standards often involves R&D.

- engaging in electronic surveillance and other *intelligence-gathering* activities to detect cyberthreats;
- engaging in investigations of cybercrime and other *law enforcement* activities;
- developing and enforcing federal *cybersecurity* regulations; and
- preparing for and engaging in *cybercombat*.

Figure 1. Simplified Schematic Diagram of Federal Agency Cybersecurity Roles

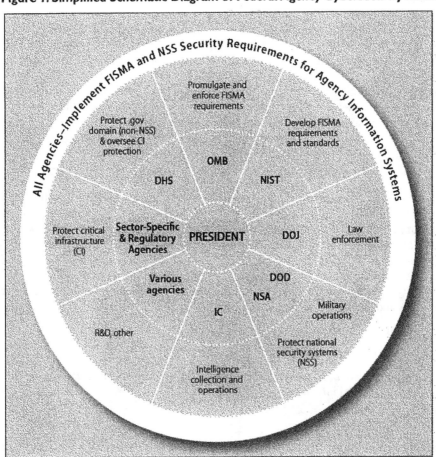

Source: CRS

Figure 1 provides a simplified schematic diagram of major agency responsibilities in cybersecurity. Below is a brief description of roles for selected agencies that may be of interest to the subcommittee, especially agencies with activities that go beyond the requirements of each to secure its own systems. The description is a highly simplified overview of major roles, drawn from various sources. It is intended to provide a basic sketch of roles and responsibilities. Because of the increasing ubiquity of information technology and its merger with communications technology, the increasing complexity of cyberspace, the continuing evolution of agency roles, and the lack of consensus about what specifically constitutes cybersecurity, among other factors, the actual distribution of responsibilities is far more complex and in some ways may be more ambiguous than what is presented here. Cybersecurity is inherently technological, and many of the activities of agencies described below are therefore related to S&T.

OMB — Office of Management and Budget. Under current law, in addition to its budgetary role in federal cybersecurity efforts, this White House office is responsible for promulgating and enforcing information security requirements under FISMA for federal information systems other than national security systems (NSS) and information systems in the Department of Defense (DOD) and Intelligence Community (IC) agencies that are crucial to their missions.

OSTP—Office of Science and Technology Policy. This White House office coordinates and facilitates interagency and multiagency cybersecurity activities, especially R&D.

NIST — National Institute of Standards and Technology. This bureau within the Department of Commerce develops the standards that OMB promulgates under FISMA. It also performs research relating to cybersecurity, develops voluntary guidance, and works with government and private-sector entities to develop cybersecurity best practices.

NSF—National Science Foundation. This independent agency funds research and education in cybersecurity, largely through academic and nonprofit institutions. NSF also provides scholarships to train cybersecurity professionals through its Scholarship-for-Service program, established administratively in 2001 under existing statutory authority and receiving specific statutory authorization in P.L. 113-274.

DHS — Department of Homeland Security. While federal responsibilities for the cybersecurity of non-NSS systems are distributed among several agencies, FISMA, as amended by P.L. 113-256, provides DHS primary responsibility for coordinating the operational security of federal systems.[5] In addition, DHS oversees federal efforts to coordinate and improve the protection of U.S. critical infrastructure (CI), most of which is controlled by the private sector. Some notable DHS cybersecurity programs and activities include the following:

- The Cybersecurity Division of the Science and Technology Directorate,[6] established in 2011, focuses on developing and delivering new cybersecurity technologies and other tools in coordination with public- and private-sector partners.

- The National Cybersecurity and Communications Integration Center (NCCIC),[7] established administratively in 2009 under existing statutory authority to provide and facilitate information sharing and incident response among public and private-sector CI

---

[5] The Obama administration had delegated such responsibilities to DHS in 2010 (Peter R. Orszag and Howard A. Schmidt, "Clarifying Cybersecurity Responsibilities and Activities of the Executive Office of the President and the Department of Homeland Security (DHS)," Office of Management and Budget, Memorandum for Heads of Executive Departments and Agencies M-10-28, July 6, 2010, http://www.whitehouse.gov/sites/default/files/omb/assets/memoranda_2010/m10-28.pdf).

[6] Department of Homeland Security, "Cyber Security Division," January 22, 2015, http://www.dhs.gov/science-and-technology/cyber-security-division.

[7] NCCIC is usually pronounced "En-kick."

entities. It received specific statutory authorization in P.L. 113-282, the *National Cybersecurity Protection Act of 2014.*

- The National Cybersecurity Protection System (NCPS) and its EINSTEIN component, which provide capabilities for intrusion prevention and detection, analysis, and information sharing for cybersecurity of federal civilian systems.

- The Enhanced Cybersecurity Services (ECS) program, established pursuant to Executive Order 13636, *Improving Critical Infrastructure Cybersecurity,* and through which DHS provides private-sector CI entities with sensitive and classified cyberthreat information either directly or through providers of commercial Internet services.

- The Continuous Diagnostics and Mitigation (CDM) program, which provides products and services to agencies to implement CDM, including sensors, tools, dashboards, and other assistance.

DOE—Department of Energy. DOE supports cybersecurity efforts in the energy sector, including electricity and nuclear, for example by assisting private-sector energy companies in developing cybersecurity capabilities for energy-delivery systems. It also provides some cybersecurity services to other agencies and private-sector entities through the DOE National Laboratories and other means. Several of DOE's 17 national laboratories also engage in cybersecurity R&D, education and training, and other activities. These include such things as modeling and simulation of systems and networks, forensic analyses, and providing test beds for investigating and improving the security of industrial control systems.

NASA—National Aeronautics and Space Administration. Most cybersecurity activities of this agency appear to be associated with protection of agency systems.

DOD — Department of Defense. DOD is responsible for military operations in cyberspace. That includes both defensive and offensive operations, with the U.S. Cyber Command, under the U.S. Strategic Command, serving as the main focus for coordinating and conducting such activities.[8] DOD agencies such as the Defense Advanced Research Projects Agency (DARPA) and the National Security Agency (NSA) also engage in cybersecurity research and development (R&D). NSA and other DOD agencies also provide assistance upon request to DHS, other civilian agencies, and private sector entities under various agreements. DOD also offers scholarship opportunities in cybersecurity at selected institutions to recruit and retain qualified personnel.

IC — Intelligence Community. The IC consists of 16 federal agencies and other entities responsible for various forms of intelligence collection and operations, including those relating to cybersecurity. The Director of National Intelligence sets standards for mission-crucial IC systems other than NSS. The Intelligence Advanced Research Projects Activity (IARPA) also engages in cybersecurity R&D.

NSA — National Security Agency.[9] While NSA is a major component of the IC, it also has a significant cybersecurity mission, serving as the designated manager of national security systems

---

[8] CRS Report R43838, *Cyber Operations in DOD Policy and Plans: Issues for Congress,* by Catherine A. Theohary and Anne I. Harrington.

[9] Administratively, NSA is part of DOD but is listed separately because of its unique cybersecurity responsibilities.

(NSS), which are information and telecommunications systems that are used in military, intelligence, and other national security activities or that handle classified information. This includes the development of security standards. NSA, along with DHS, is also involved in designation of academic centers of excellence in cybersecurity.

DOJ — Department of Justice. Most enforcement of federal criminal laws relating to cybersecurity, including investigation and prosecution, is carried out by DOJ. However, some entities within other departments also have enforcement responsibilities, such as the Secret Service in the Department of Homeland Security (DHS), and the Defense Criminal Investigative Organizations within DOD. The duties of law-enforcement agencies often involve computer forensics, electronic surveillance, and other technological activities. The Federal Bureau of Investigation (FBI) leads the multiagency National Cyber Investigative Joint Task Force (NCIJTF), which focuses on information sharing and analysis relating to cyberthreats for law enforcement purposes.

SSAs — Sector-Specific Agencies. SSAs are those federal agencies responsible for leading public/private collaborative efforts to protect the 16 designated CI sectors.[10] A plan has been developed for each sector, and many of those plans include discussion of cybersecurity concerns and activities for the different sectors.[11]

Regulatory Agencies. The regulatory environment for cybersecurity is complex, involving both technical and nontechnical activities by various agencies.[12]

Research and Development

Many federal agencies, including those discussed above, engage in R&D related to cybersecurity. Cross-agency coordination of cybersecurity R&D is the responsibility of the National Coordinating Office (NCO), under the interagency National Science and Technology Council (NSTC) of the White House. The NCO coordinates the multiagency Networking and Information Technology Research and Development (NITRD) program.[13] Agencies identifying cybersecurity R&D activities over the last three budget cycles, with funding amounts, are presented in **Table 1**.

---

[10] The White House, "Critical Infrastructure Security and Resilience," Presidential Policy Directive 21, (February 12, 2013), http://www.whitehouse.gov/the-press-office/2013/02/12/presidential-policy-directive-critical-infrastructure-security-and-resil.

[11] See Department of Homeland Security, "Sector-Specific Plans", 2012, http://www.dhs.gov/files/programs/gc_1179866197607.shtm.

[12] See, for example, Government Accountability Office, *Information Technology: Federal Laws, Regulations, and Mandatory Standards for Securing Private Sector Information Technology Systems and Data in Critical Infrastructure Sectors*, GAO-08-1075R, September 16, 2008, http://www.gao.gov/assets/100/95747.pdf. The report identified legal cybersecurity requirements associated with specific federal agencies for nine CI sectors, pertaining specifically to securing privately owned information technology systems in those sectors.

[13] CRS Report RL33586, *The Federal Networking and Information Technology Research and Development Program: Background, Funding, and Activities*, by Patricia Moloney Figliola.

Table 1. Agency Budgets for Cybersecurity and Information Assurance in the NITRD Program

Agency	Funding ($millions)		
	FY2013 Actual	FY2014 Estimate	FY2015 Request
NSF	97.9	106.6	102.5
NIST	49.7	59.7	59.7
NASA	—	—	—
DHS	75.3	77.8	67.5
DOE	32.6	36.7	30.0
DARPA	223.0	293.5	286.6
Other DOD	174.6	192.1	168.4
Other Agencies	—	—	—
Total Cybersecurity	*653.0*	*766.6*	*714.7*
Total NITRD	*3,567.6*	*3,909.4*	*3,807.2*

Source: Subcommittee on Networking and Information Technology Research and Development, Committee on Technology, *Supplement to the President's Budget for Fiscal Year 2015: The Networking and Information Technology Research and Development Program*, March 2014, https://www.nitrd.gov/pubs/2015supplement/FY2015NITRDSupplement.pdf.

Note: In addition to NASA, the other agencies reporting NITRD but not CSIA activities were the National Institutes of Health, the National Oceanic and Atmospheric Administration, the Environmental Protection Agency, the Department of Transportation, the Agency for Healthcare Research and Quality, and the National Archives and Records Administration.

Cybersecurity and Information Assurance (CSIA) is one of eight R&D topics, called Program Component Areas (PCAs), currently distinguished in the NITRD program. From FY2013-FY2015, CSIA activities accounted for about 19% of total NITRD funding. That is almost certainly an underestimate, because a significant proportion of R&D that agencies might reasonably consider related to cybersecurity may well be categorized in one of the other PCAs, such as High Confidence Software and Systems, Human Computer Interaction and Information Management, or Software Design and Productivity. Even for those agencies with no funding listed under CSIA, activities under other PCAs may well be related to cybersecurity. For example, NASA reported funding of $43.8 million in FY2013 for the other three PCAs listed above.

The CSIA activities described for each agency in **Table 1** cut across a broad range of topical areas, such as

- developing trusted computing and networking environments,
- improving the capacity of systems to evade attackers,
- improving the incentive structure for cybersecurity,
- developing better capabilities to build security into information systems,
- improving the ability to resist and recover from attacks,
- creating a more robust scientific foundation for cybersecurity,
- addressing cybersecurity priorities for CI sectors, and

- accelerating capabilities for transforming the results of R&D into usable technology and other applications.

Agencies also support and perform research on a broad array of topics aligned with their specific missions.

Cybersecurity Issues and Challenges

The risks associated with any attack depend on three factors: *threats* (who is attacking), *vulnerabilities* (how they are attacking), and *impacts* (what the attack does). The management of risk to information systems is considered fundamental to effective cybersecurity.[14]

Threats. People who perform cyberattacks generally fall into one or more of five categories: *criminals* intent on monetary gain from crimes such as theft or extortion; *spies* intent on stealing classified or proprietary information used by government or private entities; *nation-state warriors* who develop capabilities and undertake cyberattacks in support of a country's strategic objectives; "*hacktivists*" who perform cyberattacks for nonmonetary reasons; and *terrorists* who engage in cyberattacks as a form of non-state or state-sponsored warfare.

Vulnerabilities. Cybersecurity is in many ways an arms race between attackers and defenders. ICT systems are very complex, and attackers are constantly probing for weaknesses, which can occur at many points. Defenders can often protect against weaknesses, but three are particularly challenging: inadvertent or intentional acts by *insiders* with access to a system; *supply chain* vulnerabilities, which can permit the insertion of malicious software or hardware during the acquisition process; and previously unknown, or *zero-day*, vulnerabilities with no established fix.

Impacts. A successful attack can compromise the confidentiality, integrity, and availability of an ICT system and the information it handles. *Cybertheft* or *cyberespionage* can result in exfiltration of financial, proprietary, or personal information from which the attacker can benefit, often without the knowledge of the victim. *Denial-of-service* attacks can slow or prevent legitimate users from accessing a system. *Botnet* malware can give an attacker command of a system for use in cyberattacks on other systems. *Destructive* attacks can damage computers and other ICT devices, and if directed at *industrial control systems,* can result in the destruction of the equipment they control, such as generators, pumps, and centrifuges.

Most cyberattacks have limited impacts, but a successful attack on some components of CI could have significant effects on national security, the economy, and the livelihood and safety of individual citizens. Thus, a rare successful attack with high impact can pose a larger risk than a common successful attack with low impact.

Reducing the risks from cyberattacks usually involves (1) removing the threat source (e.g., by closing down botnets[15] or reducing incentives for cybercriminals); (2) addressing vulnerabilities

---

[14] See, for example, National Institute of Standards and Technology, *Managing Information Security Risk: Organization, Mission, and Information System View*, March 2011, http://csrc.nist.gov/publications/nistpubs/800-39/SP800-39-final.pdf.

[15] Botnets are basically a form of distributed computing, in which groups of computers or other Internet-enabled devices, called bots or zombies, perform automated tasks in a distributed manner over the Internet. Some bots are benign, but malicious botnets are a major cybersecurity problem. In such botnets,

by hardening ICT assets (e.g., by patching software and training employees); and (3) lessening impacts by mitigating damage and restoring functions (e.g., by having back-up resources available for continuity of operations in response to an attack).

Cybersecurity often involves highly technical measures, and the structure of ICT systems and of cyberspace is very complex. Therefore, identifying cybersecurity needs and the means to address them can be difficult. However, several near-term cybersecurity needs appear to be fairly well-established and straightforward. They include, for example,

- preventing cyber-based disasters and espionage by removing threats and hardening systems;

- reducing the impacts of successful attacks;

- improving inter- and intrasector collaboration to protect systems, particularly with respect to information sharing;

- clarifying federal agency roles and responsibilities;

- building and maintaining a capable cybersecurity workforce for both the public- and private sectors; and

- fighting cybercrime.

Many current cybersecurity activities are aimed at addressing these and related needs. More than 200 bills that would address such needs were introduced in the last three Congresses. The 113th Congress enacted five bills that arguably address aspects of several of those needs,[16] including

- amending FISMA to improve the cybersecurity of federal systems;

- updating of agency authorizations for cybersecurity R&D;

- providing for assessment of cybersecurity workforce needs at DHS and enhancing recruitment and retention capabilities; and

- providing statutory bases for a DHS information-sharing program, a NIST public/private partnership effort to develop best practices for CI cybersecurity, and an NSF program for educating cybersecurity professionals.

Bills not enacted included some that would have provided mechanisms to reduce legal and other barriers to information sharing, revised current federal cybercrime law, or provided a federal standard for notification of data breaches of data held by private-sector entities that contain the personal information of individuals.

---

devices are infected with software that allows a controller, called a botmaster or bot herder, to use the devices in an Internet network for malicious purposes, usually without the knowledge or approval of the owner of the device.

[16] In addition to P.L. 113-256, P.L. 113-274, and P.L. 113-282 discussed above, Congress also enacted P.L. 113-246, the *Cybersecurity Workforce Assessment Act,* and P.L. 113-248, the *Border Patrol Agent Pay Reform Act of 2014.* The bills both provide for assessments of the DHS cybersecurity workforce, and the latter provides DHS with new authorities to establish cybersecurity positions and set compensation for them.

The immediate and short-term needs discussed above exist in the context of more difficult long-term challenges. The existence of such challenges has been recognized by various observers over many years. For example, the 2008 Comprehensive National Cybersecurity Strategy recognized a need for the development of long-term strategic options and the need to identify "grand challenges" to address difficult cybersecurity problems.[17] The 2011 NSTC strategic plan for cybersecurity R&D recognized the need to develop cybersecurity principles that would endure changes in both technologies and threats.[18] Such challenges can be characterized in many different ways. One approach that may be useful is to characterize a particular set of difficult challenges that could be used to inform longer-term government and private-sector activities. One such set consists of four challenges: design, incentives, consensus, and environment (DICE).

Design. Experts often say that effective security needs to be an integral part of ICT design, not something that is added on toward the end of the development cycle. Yet, developers have traditionally focused more on features than security, largely for economic reasons. Also, many future security needs cannot be predicted with any certainty, posing a difficult challenge for designers.

Incentives. The structure of economic incentives for cybersecurity has been called distorted or even perverse. Cybercrime is regarded as cheap, profitable, and comparatively safe for the criminals. In contrast, cybersecurity can be expensive, is by its nature imperfect, and the economic returns on investments are often unsure. Economic incentives can be influenced by many factors, but one fundamental consideration is the degree to which users demand good cybersecurity as an essential feature of ICT systems and components.

Consensus. Cybersecurity means different things to different stakeholders, with little common agreement on meaning, implementation, and risks. Substantial cultural impediments to consensus also exist, not only between sectors but within sectors and even within organizations. Efforts such as the development of the NIST-led Cybersecurity Framework appear to be achieving some improvements in such consensus. However, one fundamental difficulty is that the increasing economic and societal prominence of cyberspace arises to a significant degree from the ability of ICT to connect things in unprecedented and useful ways. In contrast, security traditionally involves separation. Increasingly, cybersecurity experts and other observers are arguing that traditional approaches such as perimeter defense are insufficient, but consensus on a new conceptual framework has yet to emerge.

Environment. Cyberspace has been called the fastest evolving technology space in human history, both in scale and properties. This rapid evolution poses significant challenges for cybersecurity, exacerbating the speed of the "arms race" between attackers and defenders, and arguably providing a significant advantage to the former. New and emerging properties and applications—especially social media, mobile computing, big data, cloud computing, and the

---

[17] The White House, "The Comprehensive National Cybersecurity Initiative," March 5, 2010, http://www.whitehouse.gov/cybersecurity/comprehensive-national-cybersecurity-initiative.

[18] National Science and Technology Council, *Trustworthy Cyberspace: Strategic Plan for the Federal Cybersecurity Research and Development Program*, December 2011, http://www.whitehouse.gov/sites/default/files/microsites/ostp/fed_cybersecurity_rd_strategic_plan_2011.pdf.

Internet of Things—further complicate the evolving threat environment, but they can also pose potential opportunities for improving cybersecurity, for example through the economies of scale provided by cloud computing and big data analytics. In a sense, such developments may provide defenders with opportunities to shape the evolution of cyberspace toward a state of greater security.

Legislation and executive actions in the 114th Congress could have significant impacts on those challenges. For example, cybersecurity R&D may affect the design of ICT, cybercrime penalties may influence the structure of incentives, the Cybersecurity Framework may improve consensus about cybersecurity, and federal initiatives in cloud computing and other new components of cyberspace may help shape the evolution of cybersecurity.

Debate about Federal Agency Roles in Improving Cybersecurity

Ongoing debate about the proper role of government in improving cybersecurity may have significant impacts on legislative developments. In general, that debate has mirrored the broader debate about the role of government. Two examples are described below.

Cybersecurity Regulations

For example, some observers have argued that more government regulation of at least some CI sectors is important for improving their cybersecurity, both to provide incentives for implementation of effective cybersecurity measures and guidance for what kinds of protection should be implemented. Proponents have also argued, among other things, that voluntary approaches have not worked well. They also state that CI sectors and subsectors that are already regulated, in particular financial services and electric power, have been largely successful at improving their cybersecurity as a result at least in part of regulatory requirements, and that opposition to such regulations within the sectors is minimal.

Opponents of increased regulation argue, in contrast, that expanding federal requirements would be costly and ineffective, that better mechanisms exist to enhance cybersecurity, and that given the rate of change in the cyber-technology space, increased regulation would in many cases be too inflexible to be useful and may impede innovation and economic growth and the international competitiveness of American companies. In addition, some have argued that the Cybersecurity Framework may provide sufficient incentives and guidance for CI entities to improve their cybersecurity.

Under Executive Order 13636, the Obama Administration required that certain regulatory agencies engage in consultative review of the framework, determine whether existing cybersecurity requirements are adequate, and report to the President whether the agencies have authority to establish requirements that sufficiently address the risks (it does not state that the agencies must establish such requirements, however), propose additional authority where required, and identify and recommend remedies for ineffective, conflicting, or excessively burdensome cybersecurity requirements.

The assessments of regulatory requirements and proposed actions under the order focused on three agencies: DHS, the Environmental Protection Agency (EPA), and the Department of Health and Human Services (HHS). The Administration concluded that "existing regulatory requirements, when complemented with strong voluntary partnerships, are capable of mitigating cyber risks to our critical systems and information."[19]

Information Sharing

Barriers to the sharing of information on threats, attacks, vulnerabilities, and other aspects of cybersecurity—both within and across sectors—have long been considered by many to be a significant hindrance to effective protection of information systems, especially those associated with CI.[20] Examples have included legal barriers, concerns about liability and misuse, protection of trade secrets and other proprietary business information, and institutional and cultural factors—for example, the traditional approach to security tends to emphasize secrecy and confidentiality, which would necessarily impede sharing of information.

Proposals to reduce or remove such barriers, including provisions in legislative proposals in the last two Congresses, have raised concerns,[21] some of which are related to the purpose of barriers that currently impede sharing. Examples include

- risks to individual privacy and even free speech and other rights;

- use of information for purposes other than cybersecurity, such as unrelated government regulatory actions;

- commercial exploitation of personal information; and

- anticompetitive collusion among businesses that would currently violate federal law.

Research and Development

The need for improvements in fundamental knowledge of cybersecurity and new solutions and approaches has been recognized for well over a decade[22] and was a factor in the passage of the

---

[19] Michael Daniel, "Assessing Cybersecurity Regulations," *The White House Blog*, May 22, 2014, http://www.whitehouse.gov/blog/2014/05/22/assessing-cybersecurity-regulations.The document notes that the executive order does not apply to independent regulatory agencies.

[20] See, for example, The Markle Foundation Task Force on National Security in the Information Age, *Nation At Risk: Policy Makers Need Better Information to Protect the Country*, March 2009, http://www.markle.org/downloadable_assets/20090304_mtf_report.pdf; CSIS Commission on Cybersecurity for the 44th Presidency, *Cybersecurity Two Years Later*, January 2011, http://csis.org/files/publication/110128_Lewis_CybersecurityTwoYearsLater_Web.pdf.

[21] See, for example, Greg Nojeim, "WH Cybersecurity Proposal: Questioning the DHS Collection Center," *Center for Democracy & Technology*, May 24, 2011, http://cdt.org/blogs/greg-nojeim/wh-cybersecurity-proposal-questioning-dhs-collection-center; and Adriane Lapointe, *Oversight for Cybersecurity Activities* (Center for Strategic and International Studies, December 7, 2010), http://csis.org/files/publication/101202_Oversight_for_Cybersecurity_Activities.pdf. See also comments received by a Department of Commerce task force (available at http://www.nist.gov/itl/cybersecnoi.cfm) in conjunction with development of this report: Internet Policy Task Force, *Cybersecurity, Innovation, and the Internet Economy* (Department of Commerce, June 2011), http://www.nist.gov/itl/upload/Cybersecurity_Green-Paper_FinalVersion.pdf.

Cybersecurity Research and Development Act in 2002 (P.L. 107-305, H.Rept. 107-355). That law focuses on cybersecurity R&D by NSF and NIST. The Homeland Security Act of 2002, in contrast, does not specifically mention cybersecurity R&D. However, DHS and several other agencies make significant investments in it, and several of the cybersecurity bills considered by the last three Congresses would have addressed the role of DHS. About 60% of reported funding by agencies in cybersecurity and information assurance is defense-related (invested by DARPA, NSA, and other defense agencies), with NSF accounting for about 15%, and NIST, DHS, and DOE about 5%-10% each.[23]

R&D is generally regarded as one of the less contentious cybersecurity issues. Debate has generally focused on the roles of the agencies involved, priorities relating to specific R&D areas of inquiry, and what are the optimum levels of funding for federal programs.

Cybersecurity Enhancement Act of 2014 (P.L. 113-274)

The enactment of P.L. 113-274 was in many ways a culmination of legislative efforts that had begun with the 111th Congress in 2009 with the introduction and passage by the House in 2010 of H.R. 4061, a bipartisan bill with a similar name from the House Science and Technology Committee. Neither that bill nor a related bill passed by the House in the 112th Congress, H.R. 2096, received floor consideration in the Senate. In the 113th Congress, the House again passed a related bill, H.R. 756. At the end of the 113th Congress, the Senate and House both passed and the President signed S. 1353, the Cybersecurity Enhancement Act of 2014, which became P.L. 113-274. Those bills all included revisions to the Cyber Security Research and Development Act, enacted in 2002, which provided authorization for research and postsecondary education activities in cybersecurity at NSF and NIST, as well as NIST cybersecurity standards activities.

Both H.R. 756 and S. 1353 had several similar provisions:

- A requirement for a strategic plan for cybersecurity R&D to be developed under the NITRD program;

- Revisions to NIST activities associated with development of standards for federal systems;

- Revision of NIST authorities for cybersecurity R&D;

- Authorization of NSF's cybersecurity Scholarship-for-Service Program; and

- Authorization of NIST activities in the development of international cybersecurity technical standards, the development of a federal cloud-computing strategy, and R&D related to identity management.

---

[22] See, for example, National Research Council, *Trust in Cyberspace* (Washington, DC: National Academies Press, 1999), http://www.nap.edu/catalog/6161.html.

[23] The percentages were calculated from data in R&D budget crosscuts available at the Networking And Information Technology Research And Development (NITRD) Program, "Supplements to the President's Budget," *NITRD Publications*, 2014, https://www.nitrd.gov/publications/supplementsall.aspx. See also **Table 1**.

Provisions of H.R. 756 that were not included in P.L. 113-274 included authorization of NSF social and behavioral cybersecurity research, a government-wide assessment of federal cybersecurity workforce needs, and establishment of a university-industry task force in cybersecurity.

Provisions in P.L. 113-274 that were not in H.R. 756 included

- Authorization of a public-private partnership through NIST related to the one used in developing the Cybersecurity Framework;

- Authorization for interagency programs of competitions and challenges in cybersecurity aimed at recruiting talented individuals to the cybersecurity workforce and stimulating innovative R&D and applications in cybersecurity; and

- Authorization of activities by NIST in cybersecurity awareness and education related to the agency's existing NICE program.[24]

Given the recent enactment of P.L. 113-274, a substantive analysis of the impacts of the provisions would likely be premature.

---

[24] National Institute of Standards and Technology, "National Initiative for Cybersecurity Education (NICE)," January 20, 2015, http://csrc.nist.gov/nice/.

Short Narrative Biography

ERIC FISCHER is the Senior Specialist in Science and Technology at the Congressional Research. As a senior policy analyst at CRS, he provides expert written and consultative support to Congress on a broad range of issues in science and technology policy, including cybersecurity, election reform, environment, research and development, and other topics. He has authored more than 30 CRS reports and more than 100 analytical memoranda for congressional offices on those subjects and has provided analytical support to Congress on cybersecurity for more than 10 years. As a Library of Congress official, he also served as head of the former science policy division of CRS and has been active in strategic planning and other management activities at the Library.

Dr. Fischer received a Bachelor of Science degree in biology from Yale University in 1970 and a PhD in zoology from the University of California Berkeley in 1979. After a National Science Foundation Postdoctoral Fellowship at the University of Sussex in England, he joined the faculty in psychology at the University of Washington in Seattle, where he continued his research on the ecology of marine fishes. In 1987, he was selected as a Congressional Science and Technology Policy Fellow by the American Association for the Advancement of Science and worked with the Senate Budget Committee. In 1988, he became Deputy Director of the Smithsonian Tropical Research Institute in Panama. In 1990, he joined the National Audubon Society as Senior Vice President for Science and Sanctuaries. From 1992 to 1996, Dr. Fischer was Director of the Board on Biology and the Institute of Laboratory Animal Resources at the National Research Council. He has been at CRS since 2007. He also served from 1993 to 2008 as a consultant to the United States Conference of Catholic Bishops, fostering dialogue among scientific and religious leaders on topics of common interest such as evolution, environment, genetic research, and end-of-life medical care.

Chairwoman COMSTOCK. Thank you. I now recognize Mr. Dean Garfield.

TESTIMONY OF MR. DEAN GARFIELD, PRESIDENT AND CEO, INFORMATION TECHNOLOGY INDUSTRY COUNCIL

Mr. GARFIELD. Thank you, Chairwoman Comstock, Chairman Smith, Ranking Member Lipinski.

On behalf of 60 of the most dynamic and innovative companies in the world that make up the global IT sector, I would like to thank you for the opportunity to be in front of you today and to thank you as well for focusing on this issue. We think it is an issue that has the potential for bipartisan collaboration and want to seize that opportunity.

With that in mind, I would like to focus on three things: 1) how we are experiencing the cybersecurity threat today; 2) what we are doing about it; and then 3) how Congress can help. With regard to the first, as Dr. Fischer pointed out, we are living in an increasingly globally integrated and interconnected world. As a result, cyber criminals are seeking to exploit that. Gone are the days when we had intermittent viruses and instead we face a world, as my colleague Cheri McGuire pointed out, where we consistently face a threat that is increasingly global, increasingly sophisticated, and increasingly persistent. We are seeing advanced persistent threats where cyber criminals are penetrating our networks in phase, avoiding detection, and doing damage over a long period of time. As well, the threat is increasingly asymmetric and so the risks to the banking sector are often quite distinct from the risks to the manufacturing sector or the tech sector.

The reality is there is no silver bullet solution so what are we doing about it? In a word, a lot. Increasingly, our approach is based on risk mitigation and resilience. You see that both in the products that we are bringing into the marketplace, as well as the processes that we are integrating into our businesses. With the products in the marketplace, you are already seeing the results of the billions of dollars that we spend on R&D, whether that is through advanced data analytics that is allowing us to get ahead of cyber criminals or in the integration of biometrics, as you see in many of your mobile devices today, including your cell phone, which are all making a difference.

In addition to the work that we undertake with our products that are making their way into the market, we are making changes in our business processes that we would advocate for all businesses generally. One, we are increasingly making cybersecurity the default norm, so rather than turning on a cybersecurity feature, we are building products and developing systems where they come as a built-in part of the practice.

Secondly, we are increasingly relying on managed services. So rather than relying on the IT person who may or may not know anything about cybersecurity, we are relying heavily on cybersecurity professionals in carrying out work on cybersecurity within our company in network management.

As well, we are making sure that cybersecurity is a part of every aspect of our business, and with that in mind, it is worth commending NIST for the work that they have done on the cybersecurity framework, which has done a great job in making that the case for both large and small businesses.

So what can Congress do? There are four things that we would recommend. One is making sure that the laws that are on the books and our enforcement of those laws are adequate to meet the challenge and the evolving nature of that challenge that we face today.

Second, as all of the doctors on the panel have pointed out, it is important to have adequate funding for early-stage research, as well as for the work that NIST is doing to advance a framework to make it increasingly the norm for all businesses.

Third, it is important that we have legislation that helps us to disseminate cyber threat information more broadly. That is an opportunity for a bipartisan consensus in action and we hope that Congress will act on that this year.

Fourth, cybersecurity and cybersecurity risk management is not a technology issue; it is a national issue, and so it is important that all of us, including the Members of Congress, take advantage of the bully pulpit we have to educate the public about cybersecurity. So when you have your roundtables in your district, or I speak, it is important to include cybersecurity as one of the default points that we share with the public.

There is—the challenge, as all of the panelists have pointed out, is quite significant, but if we take advantage of those four steps and work collaboratively, we think there is an opportunity to make significant headway in addressing this issue. So thank you.

[The prepared statement of Mr. Garfield follows:]

Written Testimony of

Dean C. Garfield
President & CEO, Information Technology Industry
Council (ITI)

Before the

Subcommittee on Research and Technology
Committee on Science, Space, and Technology
U.S. House of Representatives

The Expanding Cyber Threat

January 27, 2015

Written Testimony of:
Dean Garfield
President & CEO, Information Technology Industry Council (ITI)

Before the:
Subcommittee on Research and Technology
Committee on Science, Space, and Technology
U.S. House of Representatives

The Expanding Cyber Threat

January 27, 2015

Chairwoman Comstock and members of the subcommittee, thank you for the opportunity to testify today. I am Dean Garfield, President and CEO of the Information Technology Industry Council (ITI), and I am pleased to testify before the Subcommittee on Research and Technology on the important topic of cybersecurity. We welcome your interest and engagement on this subject.

ITI is the global voice of the leading technology companies from all corners of the information and communications technology (ICT) sector, including hardware, software, and services—the majority of whom are based here in the United States. Cybersecurity is critical to our members' success—the protection of our customers, our brands, and our intellectual property are essential components of our business and our ability to grow and innovate in the future. Consequently, ITI has been a leading voice in advocating effective approaches to cybersecurity.

In addition, as both producers and users of cybersecurity products and services, our members have extensive experience working with governments around the world on cybersecurity policy. That's important to keep in mind because when it comes to cybersecurity, our connectedness is through an Internet that is truly global and borderless. We acutely understand the impact of governments' policies on security innovation and the need for U.S. policies to be compatible with – and lead – global norms.

I will focus my testimony on four areas: (1) The cybersecurity challenges facing our society today; (2) how industry's response to cyber threats and challenges has evolved from the start and will continue to do so; (3) how our industry sees the future of cybersecurity; and (4) how the federal government can partner with industry, or assist our work, in protecting our assets from successful cyber-attacks.

The Cybersecurity Challenges Facing Us Today

As you have heard from the other panelists, the threats and challenges are certainly many, they continually evolve, and are becoming more sophisticated.

For example, a key challenge facing us now are advanced persistent threats (APT), which use multiple phases to break into a network, avoid detection, and harvest valuable information over the long term. APTs differ from traditional threats in that they are targeted, persistent, evasive and extremely advanced. Although there are many challenges in addition to APT, there is a common theme—our cyber adversaries are becoming more and more intelligent, creative, and resourceful. These challenges do not just face American industry, but industry globally, and they impact citizens and our use of the Internet and e-commerce.

But I want to stress that not all cybersecurity threats are, or should be, of equal concern. The risks to all companies, government agencies, or citizens are inherently different because threats do not impact all of us the same way—if at all.

The risk differs by entities, depending on industry, size, and assets. Banks face different risks than manufacturers, hospitals, railroads, or movie studios. Some industries are targeted for money, others for personal data, others for confidential business information, such as trade secrets, that can help a competitor bring a product to market faster or allow them to get the upper hand in business negotiations. The threat of an organized crime syndicate seeking credit card numbers is more pertinent to an online commerce company or bank than a steel manufacturer, for example. A global bank headquartered on Wall Street will likely be a bigger target than a corner bank in a small town. Individuals at home are much less likely than companies to be the target of an advanced persistent threat. The threat may not even be a sophisticated one at all. Unpreparedness or simple error can make a gateway for the worst havoc.

When it comes to cybersecurity, one size does not fit all. The varying challenges underscore why the best approach is a system in which entities are empowered to manage their own cybersecurity risks. Each entity has a distinct risk, and needs to allocate their cybersecurity resources in their own unique way depending on what their "crown jewels" are, where they are kept, and who might want them. Our sector's innovation allows us to create products and services for all stakeholders to identify, manage, and mitigate their ever-changing risks.

ICT Industry Evolving Responses to Cyber Threats and Challenges

The ICT industry is improving cybersecurity in two distinct and important ways: via the products and services we make, and the cybersecurity risk management practices we employ and promote.

In the products and services realm, we are innovating technologies to counter and stop criminals that are increasingly able to penetrate companies' information technology (IT) systems. We are also making security easier to use and investing in managed security services. In terms of corporate cybersecurity risk management, ITI's members are major, multinational companies that have managed cybersecurity risks for decades.

Our products and services to improve security. ITI's member companies—and the global ICT industry generally—have innovated and invented security for decades. It is important to stress that the real advancements in security are not large and splashy, however. Like our bodies' immunity system, there are millions of small innovations that accumulate and come together piece-by-piece to make security more pervasive in our interconnected lives and economies. And these millions of innovations are driven by our companies, as well as thousands of new entrepreneurs and companies around the world, inventing in this space.

Like a collaborative network, the growing marketplace helps all of us deal with hackers, conduct remediation, and build skills. Enabling all of these inventions is our commitment to research and development (R&D). ITI companies invest incredible amounts in R&D. In fact, many ITI member firms have annual R&D budgets orders of magnitude greater than that of the Defense Advanced Research Project Agency (DARPA), which is renowned as our government's incubator for new technologies like networked computing. Given that DARPA's FY2014 R&D budget was $2.9 billion, our member companies are investing a staggering sum.

I am sure Members of the Committee are familiar with some of the more widely known security technologies that have evolved and captured the spotlight over the past few years. These included firewalls to protect the perimeter of your computer or network, anti-virus software to detect and remove computer viruses, and intrusion detection software (to figure out if a network had been breached), or intrusion prevention software (to try to predict and prevent being breached). These types of technologies evolved to meet changing threats and risks and continue to evolve.

Using sophisticated analytics to detect and react to anomalies. The technologies I mentioned above are just the tip of the innovation iceberg, and we are beyond the stage where firewall defenses are adequate. Each time we "up our game," hackers innovate in tandem to get around such defenses. Thus, the ICT industry has created and uses sophisticated data analytic software to monitor data, learn what is normal or aberrant, identify suspicious or anomalous activities, and react in real-time, such as by quarantining data before it can be exfiltrated. Companies also use data analytics to spot and tackle issues like fraud. And our innovations are certainly not only in products; we also innovate security services.

Making security the default norm, and easier to use. The reality is most security incidents involve some kind of human error: use of weak passwords, an employee clicking on spam and inadvertently downloading malware that hijacks a computer hard drive and exfiltrates valuable data, or inadequate network management that does not appropriately segment and section off data to those who truly need to access it.

Some of the most high profile cases over the past several months have shown how criminals are exploiting human weaknesses or mistakes made by users. One reason these mistakes happen is that security, particularly online, is difficult, complex, and time-consuming, and it is human nature to try to avoid things that are complex and take time.

To address this weak link, ICT companies are making it easier for the user to enable their own secure environments. This means we are creating products where security features such as encryption are turned on by default. Some smartphones now come with fingerprint readers in lieu of passwords to allow access. What used to be the realm of science fiction or blockbuster films are now in a phone that you can buy for a few hundred dollars.

Ensuring more experts are managing security. Our companies are also helping to make security the responsibility of experts who know how to handle it. This is happening as we migrate to managed technology services where an IT system is maintained by an outside vendor as a service-based contract, and security is built into the contracts. In the service-based world, the service provider and its cybersecurity experts remain part of that relationship and have the incentive to have a secure and resilient network. If, because of a security incident, a managed service provider's IT system is down and unable to serve customers, the provider will face financial consequences.

Our corporate cybersecurity risk management practices. ITI's members are major multinational companies that have understood and managed cybersecurity risks for decades. Our companies build risk management into their ongoing daily operations through legal and contractual agreements, cybersecurity operational controls, cybersecurity policies, procedures, and plans, adherence to global risk management standards, and many other common practices. Many operate 24-hour, 7-day-a-week network operations centers (NOCs) and participate in a host of entities that help them to understand and manage their risks, such as Sector Coordinating Councils (SCCs) and information sharing and analysis centers (ISACs). We are confident that many large, multinational companies are similar to ITI companies in these ways.

One very useful tool I want to highlight is the Framework for Critical Infrastructure Cybersecurity (Framework) released by the National Institute of Standards and Technology (NIST) in February 2014.

The Framework has great potential to help individual organizations manage their cyber risks, collectively strengthening our nation's cybersecurity. It represents an effective approach to cybersecurity because it leverages public-private partnerships, is based on risk management, and is voluntary. It references existing, globally recognized, voluntary, consensus-based standards, and best practices that are working effectively in industry now. It is technologically neutral, fostering innovation in the private sector and allowing industry to nimbly meet ever-changing cybersecurity challenges. And it nicely articulates how organizations should be factoring privacy considerations into their cybersecurity activities.

Importantly, the Framework is flexible, recognizing that different types of entities may use it for different purposes. Although it is aimed at critical infrastructure owners and operators, it can be useful to entities regardless of their size or relevance to U.S. national and economic security.

The process that went into developing this Framework has been a model for how the public and private sectors can work together to serve the national interest. In effect, the U.S. Government leveraged a tremendous amount of stakeholder input in an open, transparent, and collaborative manner, to create a major cybersecurity policy initiative. Government, industry, and other private stakeholders have a shared interest in improving cybersecurity, and the Framework moves us significantly toward that goal.

The Future of Cybersecurity and Our Top Concerns

We see the threat becoming greater and more persistent, and constantly changing. Our efforts will continue to evolve in tandem. We believe our efforts both in inventing security technologies and services, as well as in managing risks to the security of our networks, are effective approaches to cybersecurity.

But we should all be clear: there is no silver bullet to cybersecurity, and there never will be. For every new defense, there will be an adversary bent on breaching it. The beauty of technology and the Internet—that technologies and business models constantly evolve—means that targets, and attack methods, will constantly change too.

Our efforts aim to reduce the effectiveness of attack methods, and we invest in technology, processes, and education to eliminate human error as much as possible. Our goal is managing our risks and becoming resilient. And that is something we are doing very well. But this is a long journey that does not have an end.

Frankly speaking, a key concern of the ICT industry as we continue to constantly improve cybersecurity is that overbroad and inflexible policies will hamper our ability to innovate or prevent us from changing course when needed to meet dynamic threats. This isn't hyperbolic. The technology sector can point to scores of laws that were crafted in a different age that are incapable of keeping up with technology. That is not the course anyone should want when it comes to securing our connected world. In fact, the current, non-regulatory, non-prescriptive approach to cybersecurity policy in the United States that allows the most innovative minds in industry to lead and respond to the changing cyber threat is one that should not be altered.

How the Government Can Be Helpful

As policymakers, your interest in getting cybersecurity policy right is welcomed and encouraged. However, governments must resist thinking that just because there is an incident online that government must be the first responder. As I have outlined above, companies are making investments, and more and more executives are focused on solving the problems.

Working with all stakeholders, including governments, we are well-positioned to manage these risks. To compliment and enable industry efforts, U.S. government efforts should focus on:

- **Supporting federal agencies' outreach on the Framework.** ITI strongly supports the Framework for Improving Critical Infrastructure Cybersecurity, and believes Congress should allow further time for it to enhance cybersecurity practices. Congress can help the Framework achieve its goals by ensuring NIST, the Department of Homeland Security, and other relevant departments have the funding they need to conduct ongoing and extensive outreach and awareness about the Framework.

- **Continuing government funding for cybersecurity research and development (R&D).** I noted earlier that our companies invest strongly in cybersecurity R&D. We will continue to do so. But federal investments will remain essential, because we count on the government to perform R&D that simply is not viable for the private sector. By necessity, companies' R&D efforts tend to be commercially focused. We need the government to fund early-stage, high-risk research that can create breakthrough technologies and new market segments. The government can also look out over a longer time horizon, helping to set our R&D long-term sights correctly. The Cybersecurity Enhancement Act of 2014, which became law late last year, is an important down payment on government-supported R&D. For example, we look forward to reviewing the cybersecurity R&D strategic plan that will enable federal agencies to have a more unified approach to cybersecurity and information technology R&D. We hope those efforts take a similar approach to the development of the Framework by including a robust public-private engagement.

- **Continuing government efforts to raise awareness.** Government should work to raise awareness among users of technology (individuals of all ages and businesses of all sizes) about their cybersecurity risks and empower all stakeholders to understand and act upon their roles and responsibilities. In any awareness-raising, governments should partner with the private sector, which has already invested substantially in such efforts. The Cybersecurity Enhancement Act of 2014 also made strides in this area. Cybersecurity competitions and challenges for students, universities, veterans and other groups to recruit new cybersecurity talent, a cybersecurity scholarship for service program for individuals to help meet the needs of the federal government's cybersecurity mission, and the National Cybersecurity Awareness & Preparedness Program are also parts of a growing and effective education program. To meet a cyber threat that will always evolve, we need to encourage a strong workforce to bring their talents to secure our online world.

- **Passing legislation improving the government's ability to deter, investigate, and prosecute cybercrime.** While many private-sector entities are making substantive efforts to manage their risks and protect their networks, intellectual property, and businesses, criminals continually evolve their tactics and are becoming much more sophisticated. The breadth of criminal activity and number of bad actors make getting ahead of them and crafting responses to incidents difficult. Cyberspace, with its global connectivity, poses considerable challenges to those tasked with protecting it. While the tools might be different from those used by criminals offline, those who wield them are criminals nonetheless. Leveraging and strengthening these laws and enforcement capabilities of law enforcement agencies to combat cyber crime will help to increase cybersecurity.

- **Passing effective cyber threat information-sharing legislation.** Lawmakers should focus on legislation improving cybersecurity threat information sharing in a way that protects privacy and offers adequate legal liability protection for businesses.

As I noted earlier in my testimony, threats will continue to evolve, and so must our responses. Thus, there will be changing needs for education, awareness, R&D, and legislation. In order to effectively and nimbly stay ahead of the threats, Congress must approach these challenges by employing flexible, risk-based approaches that are technology-neutral and foster robust public-private collaboration.

Conclusion

Members of the subcommittee, ITI and our member companies are pleased you are examining the important issue of cybersecurity in the 21st Century. As I said at the opening of my testimony, while the challenges are many, we also have an opportunity to get it right. The ICT industry is constantly innovating and is committed to addressing those threats. We stand ready to provide you any additional input and assistance in our collaborative efforts to develop balanced policy approaches that help all of us to collectively improve cybersecurity risk management and resilience.

Thank you.

Information Technology
Industry Council

Dean C. Garfield, ITI President and CEO

Dean Garfield is the President and CEO of the Information Technology Industry Council (ITI). Since taking on this role in 2008, Dean has built ITI into a powerhouse of advocacy, insight, and influence in Washington, D.C., and throughout the world. He leads a team of professionals who, combined, bring nearly three centuries of advocacy experience to bear on the most complex policy challenges facing the world's leading technology companies.

Dean has worked to foster a policy environment that embraces cutting-edge research, game-changing technologies, and national economic champions as central to the foundation for sustained job creation and growth. The results: the tech sector has continued to grow despite global economic challenges. Companies are expanding -- putting more people to work, creating breakthrough products and services, and expanding into new markets with enormous opportunity. Under Dean's leadership, ITI has defined the tech agenda for global policymakers, expanded its membership and influence, and launched a foundation that serves as the preeminent thought leader on innovation. ITI has deepened its expertise on core issues -- from trade and new market development to taxes, from cloud computing to core standards. During Garfield's tenure, ITI's advocacy experts have helped to achieve critical legislative victories in the U.S. and internationally, knocking down barriers to innovation, strengthening America's economic competitiveness, and advancing sustainable technologies that will be at the heart of 21st century innovation.

Prior to joining ITI, Dean served as Executive Vice President and Chief Strategic Officer for the Motion Picture Association of America (MPAA). While there, he developed the association's global strategies, securing accomplishment of key operational objectives, forged industry alliances on behalf of the MPAA, and led the MPAA's Research and Technology Departments. Dean also represented the MPAA before legislative bodies and at key conferences around the world, including the European Commission and Oxford University.

Dean also served as Vice President of Legal Affairs at the Recording Industry Association of America (RIAA). He helped to develop the organization's comprehensive intellectual property policy and litigation strategies and managed several of the United States' most important intellectual property cases, including the Grokster/Kazaa case, from its filing to its resolution at the Supreme Court.

He received a joint degree from New York University School of Law and the Woodrow Wilson School of Public Administration and International Affairs at Princeton University. He was a Ford-Rockefeller as well as a Root-Tilden-Snow scholar.

In 2011, Dean was named one The Root's 100 most influential African-Americans. Dean was honored with the first REACH Breaking Barriers Award in May 2010, recognizing him for his deep commitment to leading the world's most dynamic industry in its efforts to support and inspire young people to develop the important science, technology, engineering and math (STEM) skills they must have to become tomorrow's scientific problem solvers. In addition, he is a regular contributor on the Huffington Post and has been featured in several national publications, on National Public Radio and Bloomberg Television News, representing the high-tech industry on the issues that matter most to the sector.

Information Technology Industry Council
1101 K St, NW Suite 610, Washington, D.C. 20005
T +1 (202) 737.8888   www.itic.org

Innovation. Insight. Influence.

Chairwoman COMSTOCK. I thank the witnesses for their testimony and now the Committee rules limit our questioning to five minutes and so as the Chair I will do the opening round of questions.

So actually I would like to pick up on your four points, Mr. Garfield, but have you all address. Given it is a national issue, what would you recommend that we, when we go home, that we tell people how to—you know, at our town halls, how to engage, what they can do personally at home and maybe some of these 90 percent of the breaches that we can prevent, what can we do with the public education to prevent those most common?

Mr. GARFIELD. I can start and do something quite simple, which is you have heard a lot of data around the risk that we all present because oftentimes cyber breaches are caused by human error, and so making sure that we are using multilevel authentication, for example, so not just relying simply on a password. To the extent that your technology isn't deploying cyber as a default, turning it on so that you have the benefit of all the research and development that is taking place.

The other thing that I would say is we often make common mistakes. You know, we post our passwords on our computer, and so moving away from doing things like that makes us vulnerable is an impostant part of——

Chairwoman COMSTOCK. Sort of like don't leave the keys in the car.

Mr. GARFIELD. Exactly.

Chairwoman COMSTOCK. Okay.

Ms. MCGUIRE. So there are a couple of additional things that I will add to Dean's list. The first is make sure that you are using very strong and complex passwords. You have heard a lot about the research and development going on today both within the NSF and NIST around new authentication methods and password technology but this is one of the most basic things that people can do today. Be careful when you are developing your passwords not to use things that you have posted on your social media site. What an easy way to socially engineer your password. Also make sure that you keep your security products and your systems up-to-date, keep them patched, and that will help give you quite a bit of protection, and then be aware—always be aware. Just as you are walking down the street, being aware of your surroundings, be aware of your surroundings when you are online. Be careful about accepting emails or clicking on attachments for things that you may not be sure of what they are and be very aware of that because that is the most common way of getting your computer infected is clicking on something that maybe you shouldn't have.

Chairwoman COMSTOCK. Any—sure.

Dr. KUROSE. Yes. I would like to just raise two quick points. First, in terms of what we do, certainly a sustained investment in fundamental research is incredibly important, but we need to really focus on the root causes of cybersecurity challenges, not just treating the symptoms. I mean we do need to do both but I think the need for fundamental research is critical.

And something that I think you have heard all the panelists talk about is that it is a socio-technical problem. Technology alone is not going to solve the problem. It is technology together with the correct application and the understanding of the human dimension and the social dimension of security is very important.

Chairwoman COMSTOCK. And then maybe to all of you again, how do you, as you gather this expertise and we constantly have to adapt and change, how do you prevent the person who is working with your company or working within the government today, kind of catching the bad guys and catching the cyber threats and the hacktivists, from not turning into the bad guy who is now going out with that knowledge and doing that and how do we prevent that and what kind of safety measures and processes do we have to have in place in the public sector and the private sector? I know that is pretty broad but——

Dr. ROMINE. Well, certainly I can—the insider threat is one of the most challenging things to address principally because, by definition, you are talking about someone that you view as a trusted entity so you have to be very cautious about demonstrating that you don't trust your own people, so you have to be very careful about that.

From our perspective I think we are coming to a situation where increasingly we have more tools at our disposal to do the data analytics for some of the things that are going on within an organization, and there are opportunities to detect anomalous behavior that might reveal that kind of insider threat.

Ms. McGUIRE. And I would just add to that that there are technologies out there today such as data loss prevention technologies, setting your controls appropriately within corporations and governments that will allow you to see how data traverses your network and actually alarm and trigger when your data is moving to places that it shouldn't be. So those are technologies that are very much available today and could in fact prevent a lot of bad things from happening.

Chairwoman COMSTOCK. Okay. Thank you. Thank you. And now I recognize Mr. Lipinski for five minutes.

Mr. LIPINSKI. Thank you, Madam Chairwoman. I want to thank the witnesses for their testimony and I just want to pick up on one thing that we were discussing in the Chairwoman's questions is that Dr. Kurose talked about—he said it was a socio-technical problem in terms of security, and I think that points out the importance of social science research that is done to help us better understand and to teach people how to, you know, avoid stepping into these— a lot of these cyber problems and being victims of cyber crimes.

But I wanted to—my first question I wanted to ask Dr. Kurose, Dr. Romine, and Dr. Fischer. For years we have heard from nongovernmental experts about weaknesses in interagency coordination of cybersecurity R&D. The civilian agencies with cybersecurity research programs developed a federal cybersecurity R&D strategy in December 2011. As I noted in my opening, the Cybersecurity Enhancement Act that passed last month strengthened interagency coordination in this area. And I know the Cybersecurity Enhancement Act is very new so there may or may not be anything much you can say about that.

But I want to also ask how the—how has the federal R&D strategy influenced your own agency's cybersecurity R&D portfolio and how has it strengthened interagency coordination and collaboration. Dr. Kurose?

Dr. KUROSE. Thank you. I would like to just quickly mention then the Networking and Information Technology Research and Development program, NITRD, that we talked about a little bit earlier. This provides an interagency coordination mechanism and there are specific subcommittees there, one on cybersecurity and information assurance, and that is a vehicle by which representatives from multiple agencies can get together and activities can be coordinated. And one of the co-chairs from the cybersecurity subcommittee there is from the National Science Foundation and the activities there very much find their way back into our discussions at the National Science Foundation.

Mr. LIPINSKI. Thank you. Dr. Romine?

Dr. ROMINE. Yes, I would like to echo what Dr. Kurose said about the value of having a standing interagency working group on cybersecurity and information assurance. That is one of the more robust groups I think under the NITRD program and there is a lot of conversation that takes place across federal agencies and a lot of coordination around specific topics.

There have been some strategic planning activities in the past that the interagency working group has undertaken. The agencies among the NITRD program established a senior steering group in this arena to bring together more senior people who have budget authority within their organizations to coordinate some of the investments that are being made, and so I think that has paid dividends, in particular, the emphasis on the science of cybersecurity emerged from that conversation that was taking place.

Mr. LIPINSKI. Dr. Fischer.

Dr. FISCHER. I would just like to add that certainly I think if one looks at the history of coordination across federal agencies with respect to cybersecurity, clearly there have been—that has increased. One of the questions one has to keep in mind is that coordination also has some cost associated with it. That is to say one doesn't want—potential costs I should say. One doesn't want the coordination to reduce the ability of individual agencies to invest in, you know, consensus mission goals and so that has to be taken into account. And sometimes for somebody like us looking at, you know, trying to analyze some of the interagency documents, it can be a little difficult to figure out exactly what they mean just because it is relatively complicated.

Mr. LIPINSKI. Thank you. And I want to ask Mr. Garfield and Ms. McGuire, anything quickly you could add about your view of federal cybersecurity R&D, something else that—anything else that should be done, done differently? Ms. McGuire, Mr. Garfield, whoever wants to——

Mr. GARFIELD. I wouldn't necessarily suggest that something different has to be done. I think there is research that has to occur in early stages that have impact over the long-term that the public sector is well-positioned to do, and so making sure that there is adequate funding for that innovation and R&D to occur so that we can stay ahead of the cybercriminals is critically important.

Mr. LIPINSKI. Thank you. I yield back.

Chairwoman COMSTOCK. Thank you. I now recognize Mr. Hultgren for five minutes.

Mr. HULTGREN. Thank you, Chairwoman.

Thank you all for being here. This is obviously a very important subject for us and have—I have got a lot of questions in a lot of different directions.

But first, I would like to just get a little bit of a response from you. There was some mention—I think Dr. Romine mentioned about passwords and effectiveness of passwords. It seems like there was a lot of nodding heads going on with that. To me it seems like passwords are very effective of keeping me off my own computer because I keep forgetting them. I am wondering if there could be a way that the hackers could remind me of my passwords because I keep forgetting them.

But I wonder if you could talk just a little bit more about that, of what is the next step, what is the research, where are we at on that? Specifically, is there R&D that holds promise for a better option or solutions in passwords?

Chairwoman COMSTOCK. Great question.

Dr. ROMINE. Absolutely. I can talk from the NIST perspective. We have started a program on what we call the usability of security, and usability is a scientific discipline, a quantitative discipline to determine—our mantra in this case is we want to make it easy to do the right thing, hard to do the wrong thing, and easy to recover when the wrong thing happens anyway. Those are the three principles that I like to talk about. By the way, I shamelessly stole that from a colleague.

Mr. HULTGREN. It is a good one.

Dr. ROMINE. From our perspective, we now have research results suggesting exactly as you say. We have had, for years, anecdotal evidence suggesting that passwords just don't work. We have been able to collect validated data now suggesting that when you make passwords more complex, which you have to do because if they are easy, if they are simple, then they are guessable. But if you make them too complex, then people find ways around of the security by writing them down, by storing them in plain text files and so on. So it is really sort of counter—it can be counterproductive.

The NSTIC program that NIST manages, which is a nationwide program where we have the program office, is pledged to essentially deal with this authentication problem. Password is only one way of authenticating to the system, and it is, as we know, now a pretty poor way to do it in general and yet it is ubiquitous. It is universal. And the NSTIC program is pledged to, as they say, put a stake in the heart of the password. We are trying to transition to other means but——

Mr. HULTGREN. What is your guess on when that could happen? I mean what is a timeline, possible time frame?

Dr. ROMINE. Well, the investments that have been made in pilots, and we have 13 pilots running now, sort of span from, you know, authentication through a mechanism, a token, through biometrics, through two-factor authentication I think, as Dean alluded to earlier, or as Dr. Fischer alluded to.

So I don't know the exact timeline. I know that we are making strides in that area, we are making investments, and we are making it clear that we have now validated evidence that passwords are flawed as a mechanism for authentication.

Mr. GARFIELD. Some of those technologies are already in the marketplace. I think Ms. McGuire made the point as well. I mean many of the mobile devices that are being sold today do have biometric authentication instead of passwords, and so increasingly that is being deployed commercially.

Mr. HULTGREN. Okay.

Dr. KUROSE. So if I might add that I think you really hit the nail on the head. Passwords are something that we all have to wrestle with and I think research has shown that a one-size-fits-all approach isn't really a good way to proceed forward. There has been work that looks at trying to adapt the kinds of authentication that a system is going to use to determine who the individual is; there is a research project at Berkeley going on, and also some very interesting research that went on at Carnegie Mellon about passwords in particular. Is it length, is it complexity—what are the best ways to have users work with passwords when you have password-protected systems, and then how do you feed information back to the user to help the user along?

Mr. HULTGREN. Let me switch gears real quick. As a parent, I am amazed at how quickly young people pick up on new technology. I have seen in my own office when I struggle with a new technology, I call my staff and leave them a voicemail message, wait for them to get back to me. If they can't figure it out, they text my kids and get an answer right away. But with the access kids have, there is also concern that comes with that and I just wonder if you could talk briefly about current parental control technology. Is it adequately protecting minors? I still have a 10-year-old and 13-year-old at home, as well as older kids, but concerned certainly of protection but then also something that predators are coming after them, not waiting for them to find problem areas. So I wanted to just get your thoughts of how adequate this is and what is happening there.

Ms. McGUIRE. So I will jump in on this one.

Mr. HULTGREN. Thanks.

Ms. McGUIRE. So online child safety is a critical concern that all of us have, and particularly, as you mentioned, as kids are surfing and going everywhere, it is really hard to monitor that as a parent so there are tools available. Certainly we have them in our Norton Security products. Other products out there have—give the parent to the ability to go in and type in keywords, block certain websites, and so forth. So those are there today.

Mr. HULTGREN. Do you feel like they are pretty effective in——

Ms. McGUIRE. Our customers tell us that they are effective and so we believe that they help significantly that—there.

The other part of this, though, and it goes to this socio-technological issue, is we have to start with our kids when they are first picking up a device and start training them to be careful, to be aware online, to be safe online. It has got to start immediately and also we need to include that in our school curriculum. You know, we teach kids in general safety but we don't often teach them about cybersecurity, so that is a big area that can help.

Mr. HULTGREN. I see my time is up. Thank you, Chairwoman. I appreciate your generosity.

Chairwoman COMSTOCK. Thank you. And I now recognize Mr. Moolenaar, our Vice Chairman.

Mr. MOOLENAAR. Thank you, Madam Chair. And I appreciate the testimony today.

I also wanted to follow up on some of the areas of cybersecurity with respect to our critical infrastructure, and you had mentioned earlier, you know, the area of energy, our electric grid, I would think water, our water supply. And I guess my basic question is what is the role of research in this area? How important is that? And also, if there is research done and that is applied, how much time is it good for? Is this something that, you know, it lasts for a year? Is it something—you know, what is the length of duration that information is valid?

Dr. ROMINE. So I would like to talk to the first half of that question on the protection of critical infrastructure. This is something that NIST was called upon to do in the development of the framework under the Executive Order 13636. And the way that we approached that was to hold a series of workshops around the country with the vigorous participation of industry across all of the sectors, as well as the information technology industry itself, and I know Ms. McGuire's company and Mr. Garfield's, the companies that he represents were also vigorous participants in that process. That led to a consensus document that was spearheaded principally by the private sector but with our sort of guidance with regard to what is effective as a document. So we were able to put together a framework that I think really helps to improve—or has the potential to help improve critical infrastructure cybersecurity and I think it is beginning to have that effect.

Mr. GARFIELD. And if I may add, I think the approach that was taken by NIST in putting that together is really a model for undertaking this work.

Related to the second question you asked about the time period, it is important to keep in mind that cybersecurity criminals are always adapting and evolving and so it's important that we continue this work and continue to evolve it as well.

Dr. KUROSE. So I would like to add also the notion of ''security by design'' rather than reacting to particular threats—designing security is really a first-class consideration and the systems that we are building and the components in the system that we are building are critical. I would point out—I had mentioned the collaboration NSF has with the Semiconductor Research Corporation. There the notion is that the chips that we are building we want to be able to make sure that there haven't been back doors or other malware actually inserted into the chips during the fabrication process and during the design process, so that when those chips come out we are sure that they are going to act and behave the way they are supposed to be behaving. That is an instance of security by design.

The other point I would make is critical infrastructure, it is not just social networks that affect society, but personal devices like medical devices as well, so a lot of activity is going on there also.

Dr. FISCHER. If I could just add that with respect to the question of what kinds of R&D is needed, there are many different aspects to protecting critical infrastructure—for example, control systems which we really haven't talked about today, many of which have been very much a legacy and not really designed with security in mind. And so R&D to determine what the best way is to design control systems so that they work in a highly connected environment is important. The question of to what degree you can actually separate out critical infrastructure systems from the rest of the internet is important.

And also worth noting, as some of the other witnesses have mentioned, is the importance of social and behavioral research in determining what are the best ways for operators to help protect critical infrastructure.

Mr. MOOLENAAR. I guess just one final question also is when you are working on something like this in the area of critical infrastructure, let's just say in the electric grid, how—and this gets to the question of oversight, collaboration with different agencies. You have got, you know, Homeland Security involved, you have the energy—FERC. I mean is that something that is—are you collaborating industry by industry?

Dr. ROMINE. The workshops that we undertook were in general inclusive of many different sectors. However, we have had conversations with sector-specific groups as well, and in fact, the output, the actual document or the framework itself is reliant upon much of the input that we got from these regulated sectors, including the regulators themselves who showed up at the workshops and gave us input on what could be valuable for them.

Mr. MOOLENAAR. Okay. Thank you, Madam Chair.

Chairwoman COMSTOCK. Thank you. I now recognize Mr. Newhouse for five minutes.

Mr. NEWHOUSE. First of all, thank you, Madam Chair, for allowing me to sit in on your Committee. You know, as a freshman, we had the opportunity for several sessions on cybersecurity at our orientation retreats. We learned just enough to be concerned and not enough to know what to do about it and so I appreciate the opportunity to sit here. In fact, in one of those sessions, just an hour before we sat down, my wife called me and told me someone was using our Visa card in Texas. We hadn't been to Texas in several years so we were concerned about that.

So I have a couple questions and just real quickly and I know that we are probably going to be leaving for the Floor shortly, but, first of all, last week—and since you read it in the paper it must be true—the Associated Press reported at least 50 data-mining companies are allowed to perch on the HealthCare.gov website and access personal information entered by millions of Americans who come to the website for health insurance. As you know, these data-mining companies scour the internet constantly for all kinds of information about us. Without permission or consent from those who are being spied on, they sell that information to any number of people. So perhaps Dr. Romine and Ms. McGuire, first Dr. Romine, does the NIST Cybersecurity Framework contemplate that, that a federal agency would be certified and then allow scores of data-mining companies to set up shop at a website like that and collect sensitive information?

Dr. ROMINE. It certainly does not address that very specific issue. What it does address, however, is privacy considerations in a more general context. And I think one of the things that the Framework spells out is the need for companies who are setting up cybersecurity risk management structures within their company, whether it is a 10-person company or whether it is a multibillion-dollar, multinational corporation, that they have to ensure that privacy considerations are taken into account and there are guidelines for how to do that.

So I don't have any remarks to make on the specific issues in this case, but in general, the Framework does have a pretty strong statement about privacy, and NIST has embarked on a privacy engineering research activity partly as a result of what we learned from the Framework process, that there needs to be more guidance and more tools available for people to promote privacy considerations.

Mr. NEWHOUSE. And, Ms. McGuire, if you could comment on the presence of so many of those data-mining companies and whether or not that makes the website more vulnerable to attacks.

Ms. MCGUIRE. So I can't obviously speak to the specifics of the technology of what is being used as I am not intimately familiar with the HealthCare.gov website. I do find it surprising, though, that there are that many additive websites or technologies that are able to access the data. Certainly opening up the network, that would indicate that it would provide some additional vulnerability but I don't know all the specifics so——

Mr. NEWHOUSE. Fair enough. Yeah. Then if I may, one last question, Madam Chair. And perhaps again, Ms. McGuire and perhaps Mr. Garfield, business sectors that may be most vulnerable to cyber attack and, you know, we are in Congress looking at what role government could or should play in helping protect businesses from cyber threats, could you help us a little bit, enlighten us there?

Ms. MCGUIRE. Sure. So I talked briefly about what some of our telemetry tells us about specific sectors and what—the ones that are most targeted for attacks. Interestingly enough, public sector entities, government institutions because they are such a wealth of knowledge and information. From Social Security identity numbers, all the way to healthcare to retirement benefits, these public sector websites and data repositories clearly are targeted at a very high rate.

Also, we see the banking and finance sector, pretty much anywhere that you are going to have a rich set of data, that is where the cyber criminals will target. And happy to provide and follow up but we have a pretty good list of sort of a ranking of the most targeted sectors that we see from our global telemetry.

Mr. NEWHOUSE. Maybe what can we do about that?

Mr. GARFIELD. Yeah, the one thing I would add is related to that. The reality is that criminals are looking for vulnerabilities wherever they can find them, and so to the extent that we can figure out ways of sharing the threat matrix more broadly, then I think it would be a great assistance to us. And there is already movement in Congress around advancing legislation that would deal with the sharing of cyber threat information. Passing that legislation is one very concrete thing that I think you could do in the short term.

Mr. NEWHOUSE. Thank you.

Mr. GARFIELD. You are welcome.

Mr. NEWHOUSE. Thank you, Madam Chair.

Chairwoman COMSTOCK. Thank you.

I just had one. I think we have votes so we may not get to a second round but I did have one question I wanted to follow up on.

Do you see attacks sort of—the Christmas holidays and the opportunity for financial attacks, is that a time to sort of flood the zone and have attacks—like I usually would get called—like the gentleman said, they call, hey, are you in Hawaii buying such and such? Like no, that is not me, don't okay it.

But I had a situation where after Christmas I show up in a store, my card has a problem in a department store and they said we have—we see something that you had $7,000 worth of cosmetics that you sent to California right before Christmas. No, we didn't do that. But they had not called me, which got me thinking do they target that sort of Christmas time, that rush time because they know sort of in their rush to get things through, that may be the time they weren't calling people? In this case it was the 23rd, the 24th, and the 26th but all those things were purchased and shipped. Fortunately, they took them off the card before they showed up at my home and horrified everybody but——

Ms. MCGUIRE. Yeah, so your observation is spot on in that cyber criminals will take advantage of any social activity, any major events. We saw, for example, around the Summer Olympics we saw lots of new types of scams associated with that, the World Cup, lots of new scams with that. Even the royals wedding in the U.K., there were a plethora of new online scams that were built around that knowing that people would be searching and going to websites to look up these types of current events. So, yes, in short those international events, major national holidays, et cetera, do create additional levels of risk.

Chairwoman COMSTOCK. So in terms of best practices, those kind of things should be—set off bells or time frames so that we are doing extra work in those time frames?

Ms. MCGUIRE. Yeah. You should be careful all of the time but those especially can be more intense if you will.

Dr. FISCHER. I should mention that this relates certainly to cybercrime aimed at consumers, but there is also the question about timing of cyber attacks aimed at, say, critical infrastructure, and one of the sort of hallmarks of cyber criminals who are interested or spies who are interested in, say, getting proprietary information, intellectual property information, national security secrets, or whatever is that they will try to target a system in such a way that they can get in, exfiltrate the information, and then get out without anybody knowing. So it is common—one of the sort of common assessments is that businesses can often take months before they actually realized that they have been the victim of a successful cyber attack and it can just take hours to exfiltrate the information. So to a certain extent, with respect to—as I say, it really depends on the importance of the timing really depends on what the sector is that is being targeted.

Mr. GARFIELD. If I could add, too, just some things that Congress can do very concretely around this question, one is making sure that there adequate resources to address the criminals, right, because if it is viewed as a crime without a penalty, then people will be incentivized to continue to do it. The second is you make the point that you would normally—in the normal course be warned about it, but during that period of time, it wasn't, making sure that there are adequate resources around R&D so that the technologies that are being deployed that detect abnormal behavior are widely distributed. And so those are two things that Congress can do that can be helpful in this area.

Chairwoman COMSTOCK. And then how do we—because, you know, the concerns of privacy, you know, people—you always appreciate when you get that phone call but then the next question is, well, how do you know where I am and what I am buying? It gives people a bit—but obviously in this case I was lucky they took it all off my credit card. You know, how do they balance that?

Ms. MCGUIRE. So today there are mostly algorithms that are all predominantly——

Chairwoman COMSTOCK. Right.

Ms. MCGUIRE. —done by the machines themselves to catch those exact kinds of flags if you will of unusual behavior or unusual activity. And then of course you end up getting a phone call from a real person hopefully to——

Chairwoman COMSTOCK. So part of the public education that we do with the public is we need to separate the algorithms and the patterns that you are looking at there are separate from, say, when Google is getting all of our HealthCare.gov information. So there—these are two—they often get lumped together whereas it is two very separate things. This is the machine kind of going through data, not looking at what I am buying at the department store, just flagging things as opposed to somebody getting my data and knowing when I am on a particular site and that getting pushed out somewhere. So those are two very different types of situations, right?

Mr. GARFIELD. You could have a whole hearing around data analytics. I am not suggesting—necessarily suggesting it but you make a very good point that often people will hear big data or data analytics and think that it is personal to them. In almost all instances what is happening, there are computers that are looking at patterns and then not looking at individuals or individual data, and based on normal patterns, then passing that on to someone else. And so in this instance and in most instances it is actually an advancement that we want to see because in the end it helps us in society.

Chairwoman COMSTOCK. Right. Thank you.

And, Mr. Lipinski, did you have additional questions?

Mr. LIPINSKI. Yeah, thank you, Madam Chair. I think this will be probably quick.

I just wanted to get back to HealthCare.gov, and my understanding is that companies are not actually perched on the HealthCare.gov but they are receiving—they are being given data from there. Now, that is very different. It is still, I understand, a privacy issue, which is something certainly Congress can look at that, but as Mr. Garfield was talking about data analytics, that is a whole different issue, certainly something that, you know, we should be always concerned about privacy.

But I want to ask Dr. Romine, HealthCare.gov is FISMA-compliant. Could you just tell us what that means, what the FISMA standards are and how federal agency computer systems are—become FISMA-compliant?

Dr. ROMINE. Sure. The Federal Information Security Management Act, or FISMA, provides NIST the opportunity to develop a collection of standards and guidelines that are used by federal agencies to secure their information systems. We do that in a collaborative way with private sector involvement to try to understand exactly what the right approach is for securing those systems. What we don't really have very often is insight into that because we don't have an operational role; we have a guidance role. We don't have insight into how federal agencies are doing—are complying with FISMA requirements or FISMA guidelines.

And so in the case of HealthCare.gov, for example, I have no direct information about the actual implementation of the FISMA guidelines but it is predicated on taking cybersecurity in a risk management approach, in an analogous way to what we did with the framework for critical infrastructure cybersecurity improvement. And so the idea is to identify the risks associated with the system and a catalog of risks and a catalog of mitigations to adopt steps that are necessary to mitigate those risks and then assess the level of risk that the individual organization that is appropriate for that organization or for that particular system. So that is the approach that is taken, but as I say, with regard to any specific agency, it is really the CIO responsibility along with the Inspector General who follows up on ensuring that the guidelines are met.

Mr. LIPINSKI. Thank you very much. I don't want in any way my statements or questions to suggest that everything is wonderful with HealthCare.gov or especially the D.C. website, which was completely atrocious once again for the second year in a row as we had to deal with that being in the system this year. But I think the important thing is looking here at security and, you know, we—as I said, privacy is another issue but the security is some-thing that I think we have talked about here and had hearings here and have not found any issues with that. So thank you very much.

Chairwoman COMSTOCK. Okay. I believe, Mr. Newhouse, you wanted an additional question?

Mr. NEWHOUSE. Well, I certainly could. We could talk about some of these things for a long time but I guess following up a little bit, Dr. Romine—and I hope you don't feel picked on today, but——

Dr. ROMINE. Quite all right.

Mr. NEWHOUSE. —that is the risk you take.

Dr. ROMINE. That is right.

Mr. NEWHOUSE. You do play an important role, though, with regard to FISMA and it is—you talked a little bit about that role in your work up-to-date. I just wanted to know if there are any recommendations that you might have that would be valuable to us in any changes to the law?

Dr. ROMINE. Well, certainly I don't have any changes to the statutes to recommend. I would—it will at least give me the opportunity to thank this Subcommittee and the Committee for the work that we have done collaboratively. We have had a really good working relationship between NIST and the Subcommittee and Committee over time and we appreciate that.

I think we are in a good spot with regard to a few things. One is the FISMA risk management framework is really an important—it provides an important understanding of the appropriate balance between ensuring the ability of the private sector to innovate in this space and provide new services while at the same time maintaining an overall approach that balances that against the associated risks. And because the information technology space is so dynamic, the risk management framework is also very adaptive and dynamic as well. And so I think it is the appropriate mechanism. I appreciate the support.

Mr. NEWHOUSE. And the Congress must be just as dynamic then?

Dr. FISCHER. If I may just mention with respect to FISMA implementation, the last Congress enacted, as was mentioned, the Federal Information Security Modernization Act of 2014, and that act gave statutory authority to DHS for some operational aspects of helping to ensure that agencies have adequate cybersecurity. The Obama Administration had administratively delegated it, but previous to that the responsibilities lay entirely with OMB, which doesn't have operational capabilities. So it remains to be seen to what extent the changes in the law will lead to improvements in agencies' cybersecurity. Certainly DHS has a number of programs and activities that are aimed at that.

Chairwoman COMSTOCK. Okay. Well, I want to thank the witnesses for their very valuable testimony and we so appreciate all of your expertise, both the public sector and the private sector, and all that you are doing to bring that information to us and to the public, and we look forward to continuing to work with you. And I thank all the Members for their questions.

And I do want to note that the record will remain open for two weeks for additional comments or any information you would like to provide and any written questions from the Members. So the witnesses are now excused and this hearing is adjourned. Thank you very much.

[Whereupon, at 3:28 p.m., the Subcommittee was adjourned.]

Appendix I

ANSWERS TO POST-HEARING QUESTIONS

Responses by Ms. Cheri McGuire
HOUSE COMMITTEE ON SCIENCE, SPACE, AND TECHNOLOGY
SUBCOMMITTEE ON RESEARCH AND TECHNOLOGY

"The Expanding Cyber Threat"

Ms. Cheri F. McGuire, Vice President, Global Government Affairs & Cybersecurity Policy,
Symantec Corporation

Questions submitted by Rep. Barbara Comstock, Chairwoman, Subcommittee on Research and
Technology

1. How might U.S. industry be impacted if other countries do not adopt similar approaches to cybersecurity as the U.S.? How can we ensure that there will be a balance between legitimate risk reduction efforts and the ability of U.S. businesses to compete globally?

It is important that all countries (including the United States) adopt cybersecurity policies that recognize that cybersecurity is a global issue and that the world economy is inexplicably intertwined. Good policy encourages innovation and is both flexible and technology neutral. Rigid mandates and technology-specific solutions will not keep up with the pace of change in the technology sector and will stunt economic growth and technical innovation. Any new best practices or standards should reflect the global nature of cybersecurity and incorporate the best-in-class approaches from around the world, not just from one specific country or region. The National Institute of Standards and Technology's Cyber Security Framework (CSF), developed by industry and government in 2014 and in which Symantec was an active contributor, is a great example of such an approach. The CSF does not mandate any one approach to cybersecurity, but instead allows an organization to select the course that best fits its risk management needs.

Government surveillance revelations over the past two years have eroded confidence in US ICT companies competing overseas, and it is important that our government's approach to cybersecurity does not exacerbate this. In particular, any new legislation addressing information sharing must include: strong privacy protections; place a civilian agency at the forefront of any sharing program; and require companies that share information to minimize personally identifiable information. Good policy can drive security adoption and promote global competition.

2. Excellent security does not necessarily equate to privacy, it just means the data is safer. How do we ensure our discussions about security also incorporate privacy? Thinking especially about how often children and students are accessing networked information technology, how can parents really know what information is available online directly pertaining to their children? How can they work to secure and maintain the privacy of that information?

In the digital age, there is no privacy without security. Yet, there is an important balance between improving data security while still respecting privacy. The threshold for any discussion about security is recognizing these realities – it is naïve and unrealistic to believe that we can have privacy without security, yet we must recognize that security measures too have their limits. Parents are especially challenged in protecting their children online, as children are often the earliest adopters of new technologies and forms of communication. As such, even the most tech-savvy parent is often playing catch-up with his or her kids. Ensuring the online security of our children starts with communication – talk to them about the good things they can do and learn online, but also about the potential risks. Try to make sure that what they're doing and seeing is age-appropriate. But there are also technological aids – most modern security suites will protect your children against hackers and criminals who would compromise their devices, and also include tools that allow parents to limit the sites their kids can visit or monitor for inappropriate content.

There are also organizations that are dedicated to child online safety and that have resources available to parents. The Family Online Safety Institute (FOSI) Good Digital Parenting initiative is an excellent resource for parents who want to confidently navigate the online world with their kids. For Symantec's part, we offer technology solutions and resources for children's online safety through our Norton Family initiative. Taken together, strong communication, education, and good security tools will go much of the way to keeping kids safe online.

Responses by Dr. James Kurose

HOUSE COMMITTEE ON SCIENCE, SPACE, AND TECHNOLOGY
SUBCOMMITTEE ON RESEARCH AND TECHNOLOGY

"The Expanding Cyber Threat"

Dr. James Kurose, Assistant Director, Computer and Information Science and Engineering
Directorate, National Science Foundation

1. **Question for the Record – from Chairwoman Barbara Comstock:** *Microchip design today is incredibly complex. Thanks to this complexity, it is nearly impossible to test a chip for malicious hardware… What research does NSF perform in the realm of hardware attacks? How can companies build privacy and security into hardware so instead of being a risk for the consumer, it becomes a safeguard?*

NSF has a long history of supporting fundamental research on the security of hardware, enabling protections against vulnerabilities in hardware and product supply chains with new approaches for the detection of Trojans; protections against counterfeiting of integrated circuits; and new tamper-resistant security primitives for hardware systems.

Computing processors meet a tremendously wide range of needs, from leading-edge processors that are the "brains" behind critically-important systems and infrastructure, including networking and communications, electric power grids, finance, military, and aerospace systems, to smaller embedded processors, sensors, and other electronic components that provide "smart" functionality in a variety of applications, such as automotive braking and airbag systems, personal healthcare, industrial controls, and the rapidly growing list of connected devices often called the "Internet of Things." The wide range of devices and applications together with the exponential growth of the number of connected "things" has made security and trustworthiness of processors a critical concern. Indeed, as information and systems are increasingly connected, and are increasingly composed of software and hardware produced by global supply chains, the opportunities for malicious insiders to cause damage increases, and the risks of information leaks multiply.

Design and manufacture of today's complex hardware systems requires many steps and involves the work of hundreds of engineers, typically distributed across multiple locations and organizations worldwide. Today, semiconductor circuits and systems are designed so as to make it feasible or easier to verify, manufacture and test during subsequent steps. However, what is needed is an understanding of how to design for assurance, with the objective of decreasing the likelihood of unintended behavior or access, increasing resistance and resilience to tampering and counterfeiting, and improving the ability to provide authentication in the field. Designing for assurance requires new strategies for architecture and specification, and tools for synthesis, physical design, test, and verification, especially in design stages where formal methods are currently weak or absent. It is imperative to develop a theoretical basis for hardware security in order to design systems that are free of vulnerability and that are assured and resilient against attacks, even vulnerabilities and attacks that are not (yet) known.

As I noted in my oral testimony, NSF has worked closely with the Semiconductor Research Corporation (SRC), the world's leading technology research consortium consisting of member companies and university research programs across the globe, in the area of hardware security, with a particular focus on designing for assurance, as described above. Through the *Secure, Trustworthy, Assured, and Resilient Semiconductors and Systems (STARSS)* perspective within NSF's Secure and Trustworthy Cyberspace program, NSF and SRC are funding innovations in hardware security and facilitating close collaborations between academic researchers and industry. NSF and SRC jointly funded nine projects in FY 2014 spanning these areas; additional awards are anticipated in FY 2015. The projects funded in FY 2014 include the following:

- *IPTrust: A Comprehensive Framework for IP Integrity Validation* (Case Western Reserve University) – Modern chips include Intellectual Property (IP) blocks, or previously designed components of logic or data, from a variety of sources. This research project evaluates IP blocks to develop a framework for IP block trust analysis and verification, and develops tests to detect deeply embedded malicious changes to chip designs.

- *Combatting Integrated Circuit Counterfeiting Using Secure Chip Odometers* (Carnegie Mellon University) – This research aims to detect counterfeit integrated circuits (ICs) through Physically Unclonable Functions (PUFs) that are analogous to unforgeable Vehicle Identification Numbers (VINs) on automobiles, and also to detect used ICs through a secure chip "odometer" that is akin to vehicle odometers.

- *Trojan Detection and Diagnosis in Mixed-Signal Systems Using On-The-Fly Learned, Precomputed and Side Channel Tests* (Georgia Institute of Technology) – Trojan horses in hardware can cause integrated circuits to fail in the field. This project uses both pre-computed and dynamically generated tests to detect Trojans by using learning algorithms to refine tests in the field.

2. **Question for the Record – from Chairwoman Comstock:** *Excellent security does not necessarily equate to privacy, it just means the data is safer. How do we ensure our discussions about security also incorporate privacy? Thinking especially about how often children and students are accessing networked information technology, how can parents really know what information is available online directly pertaining to their children? How can they work to secure and maintain the privacy of that information?*

NSF agrees completely about the importance of information privacy research. In a recent NSF Dear Colleague Letter (NSF 14-021), we noted:

> "Privacy is a major issue of the information age. Organizations are increasingly acquiring and storing vast quantities of information about individuals. In addition, advances in big data analytics enable organizations to combine previously distinct information sources and to examine these data to uncover hidden patterns, correlations, and other revealing information. Research on privacy is needed to address how technological change and societal trends are combining to reshape privacy and the implications of such reshaping.

The directorates for Social, Behavioral, and Economic Sciences (SBE) and Computer and Information Science and Engineering (CISE) invite investigators to submit proposals that address the need to develop new and deeper understandings of privacy in today's networked world."

The goal of privacy research, then, is to pursue approaches that protect a person's information. For example, as I noted in my testimony, as computers are embedded everywhere, from the cash register in the coffee shop to sensors in highways, actuators in medical devices, and controls in manufacturing plants, the threat landscape for one's privacy is expanding. Tire pressure sensors installed to help drivers avoid dangerous tire under- or over-inflation can be remotely identified, thus allowing a stalker to inconspicuously track movements of potential victims or allowing criminals to track undercover law enforcement officers around a city. Beyond computer virus infections that have disabled operating room computers, hospitals have been victim to breaches of patient records. Recent studies show that a large fraction of hospital equipment is vulnerable to computer attacks[1]. Deliberate and seemingly reasonable security measures can also backfire. GoGo Inflight, which provides WiFi access on airplanes, replaced digital certificates used to prove the identity of websites with its own certificates[2], allowing it to decrypt network traffic and prevent video streaming that would interfere with throughput for other passengers. As a side effect, however, sensitive email traffic could be decrypted before it leaves the airplane, and then re-encrypted, introducing risks for those using the airplane's wireless services. Attackers could employ the same strategy by placing open "hotspots" at coffee shops. While such a cyber threat is easily detectable and circumvented, it requires technical understanding by users who are used to clicking "yes" to messages.

NSF's investments in privacy research have led to a number of important contributions in recent years, including:

- Formal methods and software analyses that further the science of privacy via principled techniques for the specification, design and analysis of privacy-aware software programs, and for formalizing and enforcing privacy and accountability in web- and cloud-based systems;
- Differential privacy techniques that aim to provide actionable global, statistical information about sensitive data, while preserving the privacy of the users whose information is contained in the data set; and
- Usable security and privacy measures that explore ways to improve warning messages, privacy settings, security interfaces and primitives based on the how end users intuitively respond to such stimuli.

In FY 2014, NSF invested approximately $25 million to support privacy research as an extension of security, including exploring basic privacy constructs and their application in many areas of information technology. NSF's privacy support is largely driven bottom-up by research proposals from the academic research community, including through the *Trustworthy Computing* perspective within the Secure and Trustworthy Cyberspace program. Projects range in size from

---

[1] http://www.wired.com/2014/04/hospital-equipment-vulnerable/
[2] http://arstechnica.com/security/2015/01/gogo-issues-fake-https-certificate-to-users-visiting-youtube/

disciplinary research that recognizes the responsibilities of the government, the needs of society, and opportunities for innovation in the digital realm. As part of this effort, the CSIA R&D SSG published a Request for Information in September 2014[3]. On the basis of this input[4], the CSIA R&D SSG convened a cross-sector workshop in February 2015 to identify key privacy perspectives, needs, and challenges that should be considered in forming a privacy research strategy; to gain a better understanding of what objectives should guide federal privacy research; and to examine prospective research themes that might be used to organize and prioritize federal research in privacy. The workshop, which spanned government, academia, industry, individual, and societal perspectives, will lead to a report that decomposes privacy into areas where goals for privacy research could be established; creates a framework that links privacy research objectives into a coherent picture; and formulates research objectives in ways that invite a variety of contributions and approaches from many disciplines.

---

[3] https://federalregister.gov/a/2014-22239
[4] https://www.nitrd.gov/cybersecurity/nationalprivacyresearchstrategy.aspx

HOUSE COMMITTEE ON SCIENCE, SPACE, AND TECHNOLOGY
SUBCOMMITTEE ON RESEARCH AND TECHNOLOGY

"The Expanding Cyber Threat"

Dr. James Kurose, Assistant Director, Computer and Information Science and Engineering
Directorate

Questions submitted by Rep. Elizabeth Esty, Subcommittee on Research and Technology

1. *Many experts testifying before our Committee have agreed that humans are one of the weakest links in maintaining cybersecurity for both individuals, and our nation. In fact, a password management company recently released a study that found the most common passwords in the United States are "123456" and "password." Given how critical the human factor is in maintaining cyber security, can you expand on the role that NSF's Social, Behavioral, and Economic Sciences directorate plays in NSF's cybersecurity research agenda? What are some of the basic questions that behavioral and social scientists are pursuing that may contribute to our cybersecurity?*

With the rapid pace of technological advancement, we are witnessing the tight integration of financial, business, manufacturing, and telecommunications systems into a networked, global society. These interdependencies can lead to vulnerabilities and threats that challenge the security, reliability, and overall trustworthiness of critical infrastructure and the systems that people depend on and use every day. The result is a dramatic shift in the size, complexity, and diversity of cyber attacks.

In response to these changing threats, NSF has long supported fundamental cybersecurity research, resulting in many powerful approaches deployed today. NSF continuously brings the problem-solving capabilities of the Nation's best minds to bear on these challenges; it also promotes connections between academia and industry.

And projects are increasingly interdisciplinary, spanning computer science, mathematics, economics, behavioral science, and education. They seek to understand, predict and explain prevention, attack and defense behaviors, and contribute to developing strategies for remediation, while preserving privacy and promoting usability.

Indeed, as you note, there is increasing recognition that we need improved methods for building socio-technical systems that perform as intended, even in the face of threats. NSF's portfolio includes projects studying security in human-centric systems and in a variety of web-application contexts as well as in smartphones, voting systems, medical devices, automotive systems, and other cyber-physical systems. New methods explore how to effectively communicate security and privacy information to users in ways that they can better understand, and offer approaches for blind users to receive useful but unobtrusive security information, since "pop up" warnings are ineffective. Collaborations between computer scientists and social scientists continue to expand the scope of how we understand security problems and their solutions.

Since FY 2012, NSF's Secure and Trustworthy Cyberspace program has sought to secure the Nation's cyberspace from multiple perspectives. A key perspective is that of social, behavioral, and economic sciences, and aims to understand, predict, and explain prevention, attack and/or defense behaviors and contribute to developing strategies for remediation. Research that contributes to the design of incentives, markets, or institutions to reduce either the likelihood of cyber-attack or the negative consequences of cyber-attack are especially encouraged, as are projects that examine the incentives and motivations of individuals.

Let me highlight the results of two projects exploring socio-technical aspects of the cyber security challenge:

- *Beyond Technical Security: Developing an Empirical Basis for Socio-Economic Perspectives* (University of California at San Diego, International Computer Science Institute, and George Mason University) – This interdisciplinary team has sought to take a broader socio-economic view of cyber security to enable a more effective basis for designing security interventions. To date, the researchers have developed a classifier that will soon be integrated by Twitter to identify possible fraudulent Twitter accounts at the time when they are being registered by cybercriminals; and characterized the scale and complexity of the spam ecosystem, and worked closely with merchant banks to shut these down.

- *An Empirical Study of Text-based Passwords and Their Users* (Carnegie Mellon University) – The goal of this project was to research how passwords are created, how they resist hacking, and how usable they are. The project found that password-composition policies that emphasize length requirements rather than complexity often result in passwords that are both more secure and more usable. The use of password meters during password creation reliably led to stronger passwords without impact on usability. The researchers also found that detailed, step-by-step guidance has the potential to help users but can also cause lower user engagement, hurting security; on the other hand, detailed, specific feedback generally helped users create strong and easy-to-use passwords.

Beginning in FY 2013, NSF's Directorates for Computer and Information Science and Engineering (CISE) and Social, Behavioral and Economic Sciences (SBE) jointly authored a Dear Colleague Letter to accelerate progress in this interdisciplinary area by encouraging new collaborations between computer scientists and social, behavioral and economic scientists. The 2014 Dear Colleague Letter (NSF 14-021) noted:

> "The directorates for Social, Behavioral, and Economic Sciences (SBE) and Computer and Information Science and Engineering (CISE) invite investigators to submit proposals that address the need to develop new and deeper understandings of privacy in today's networked world. Our interest spans both disciplinary and interdisciplinary research in an array of SBE sciences. Proposals for workshops to explore novel and interdisciplinary SBE and SBE/CISE approaches to privacy are also welcome."

We have continued this DCL in FY 2015. To date, over 25 interdisciplinary awards have been funded, including the following:

- *The Game Changer: A New Model for Password Security* (Cleveland State University) – Most existing passwords are based on either text or patterns (e.g., a swipe pattern on a touchscreen smartphone). This collaboration between an electrical engineer, a sociologist, and a psychologist explores password schemes based on remembering layouts of pieces on a board game (e.g., chess, Monopoly), which are both more memorable than random strings of characters, and also more secure because users will not write them down.

- *Investigating Elderly Computer Users' Susceptibility to Phishing* (University of Colorado at Colorado Springs) – Existing studies have evaluated younger users' susceptibility to phishing attacks, but have not paid sufficient attention to elderly users' susceptibility to phishing in realistic environments. Seniors have become very attractive targets for online fraud. This collaboration between a computer scientist and a psychologist compares younger and older computer users' susceptibility to both the traditional and the newly emergent single sign-on phishing campaigns.

- *Consumer Response to Security Incidents and Data Breach Notification* (Carnegie Mellon University) – When customers receive notification of a breach of personal data, they may take advantage of the free notification frequently provided. But what is unclear is whether their behavior changes: do they change their buying habits with the merchant? This collaboration between a management science professor and a robotics professor uses a Big Data approach to determine how real users respond to reports of identity theft. Through cooperation with a major bank that has suffered data breaches, the researchers are able to establish the ground truth of how users behave when their data has been stolen, by specifically comparing behaviors of customers who have been notified that their data were breached to those whose data have not been breached.

Across its cyber security research and development programs, NSF continues to cast a wide net and let surface the best ideas for this socio-technical system, such as those highlighted above, rather than pursuing a prescriptive research agenda. It engages the cyber security research community in developing new fundamental, long-term, often interdisciplinary or multi-disciplinary ideas, which are evaluated by the best researchers through the merit review process. This process, which supports the vast majority of unclassified cyber security research in the U.S., has led to innovative and transformative results.

Responses by Dr. Charles H. Romine

HOUSE COMMITTEE ON SCIENCE, SPACE, AND TECHNOLOGY
SUBCOMMITTEE ON RESEARCH AND TECHNOLOGY

"The Expanding Cyber Threat"

Dr. Charles H. Romine, Director, Information Technology Laboratory, National Institute of
Standards and Technology

Questions submitted by Rep. Barbara Comstock, Chairwoman, Subcommittee on Research and
Technology

1. Microchip design today is incredibly complex. Thanks to this complexity, it is nearly
   impossible to test a chip for malicious hardware. What is NIST doing to ensure that hardware
   doesn't present a serious cyber risk? What research does NSF perform in the realm of
   hardware attacks? How can companies build privacy and security into hardware so instead of
   being a risk for the consumer, it becomes a safeguard?

Response:
What is NIST doing to ensure that hardware doesn't present a serious cyber risk?
**NIST is working in areas of Supply Chain Assurance including hardware and conducting
research into methods for hardware testing. There are significant efforts in this area
from government, industry and academic research for the purposes of identifying
maliciously tampered hardware to identifying counterfeit and cloned hardware in order
to assure that these items meet requirements and provide a secure and stable
environment.**

How can companies build privacy and security into hardware so instead of being a risk for the
consumer, it becomes a safeguard?

**Companies are building security and privacy capabilities into hardware today. Trusted
Platform Modules (TPMs), Hardware Assisted Security, Hardware Cryptographic
Modules and Hardware Trusted Execution Technology are just a few examples of
current technologies that are available to reduce risks to consumers.**

2. Excellent security does not necessarily equate to privacy, it just means the data is safer. How
   do we ensure our discussions about security also incorporate privacy? Thinking especially
   about how often children and students are accessing networked information technology, how
   can parents really know what information is available online directly pertaining to their
   children? How can they work to secure and maintain the privacy of that information?

Response:
**Privacy and security are complementary and supporting efforts but, as you correctly state,
one does not equate to the other. NIST is the leader and convener for the National
Initiative for Cybersecurity Education (NICE) which works in a multi-agency, multi-
stakeholder collaboration to bring awareness of privacy issues to children, parents and
care givers and to share training, tools and best practices for both securing information
and ensuring the privacy of children and individuals. NIST is also conducting research
into Privacy engineering to design and develop technical references for systems to have
capabilities to protect and enhance privacy.**

Question for the Record

Question

Excellent security does not necessarily equate to privacy, it just means the data is safer. How do we ensure our discussions about security also incorporate privacy? Thinking especially about how often children and students are accessing networked information technology, how can parents really know what information is available online directly pertaining to their children? How can they work to secure and maintain the privacy of that information?

Response

To ensure that discussions about security incorporate privacy, it is important to understand the relationship between the two concepts. Both are complex, with varying interpretations among different observers and different circumstances. This discussion will focus on cybersecurity in the sense of information security in cyberspace. Information security is defined in the Federal Information Security Management Act (FISMA) as

> protecting information and information systems from unauthorized access, use, disclosure, disruption, modification, or destruction in order to provide—
> (A) integrity, which means guarding against improper information modification or destruction, and includes ensuring information nonrepudiation and authenticity;
> (B) confidentiality, which means preserving authorized restrictions on access and disclosure, including means for protecting personal privacy and proprietary information; and
> (C) availability, which means ensuring timely and reliable access to and use of information.[1]

The meaning of privacy differs depending on context as well. It can refer to the degree of control an individual has over personal information and decisions, protection of personal information from public or government scrutiny, or related matters. In some contexts, consideration may be limited to information that is sufficient to identify an individual. The term "personally identifiable information" (PII) refers to this aspect of privacy and has been defined by the Office of Management and Budget (OMB) as

> information which can be used to distinguish or trace an individual's identity, such as their name, social security number, biometric records, etc. alone, or when combined with other personal or identifying information which is linked or linkable to a specific individual, such as date and place of birth, mother's maiden name, etc.[2]

The Federal Trade Commission (FTC) has expressed concern about and provided guidance on online privacy for 20 years. It developed a set of four principles, called the Fair Information

---

[1] 44 U.S.C. §3552.

[2] Clay Johnson, "Safeguarding Against and Responding to the Breach of Personally Identifiable Information," Memorandum for the Heads of Executive Departments and Agencies, M-07-16, (May 22, 2007), http://www.whitehouse.gov/sites/default/files/omb/memoranda/fy2007/m07-16.pdf.

Practice Principles, or FIPP, focusing on processes for addressing concerns about control of personal information:

1. **Notice.** Data collectors must disclose their information practices before collecting personal information from consumers;

2. **Choice.** Consumers must be given options with respect to whether and how personal information collected from them may be used for purposes beyond those for which the information was provided;

3. **Access.** Consumers should be able to view and contest the accuracy and completeness of data collected about them; and

4. **Security.** Data collectors must take reasonable steps to assure that information collected from consumers is accurate and secure from unauthorized use.[3]

Those principles have also been adopted by other federal agencies in addressing issues relating to privacy.[4]

Such complexity can complicate debate about federal policies relating to privacy. In addition, the concept is not static but rather evolving in the face of the continuing evolution of cyberspace. One way to characterize privacy more simply is to use it in the sense of an individual's control over access to and use of personal information by others, and that is how it is used in this response.[5]

Cybersecurity is sometimes conflated inappropriately in public discussion with privacy and other concepts such as information sharing, intelligence gathering, and surveillance. Such conflation can be mitigated by distinguishing the two main ways that privacy and cybersecurity are related:

1. *Good security is essential to privacy protection in cyberspace.* That is clear from the inclusion of confidentiality as one of the three pillars of the definition of information

---

[3] Federal Trade Commission, *Privacy Online: Fair Information Practices in the Electronic Marketplace,* Report to Congress, (May 2000), https://www.ftc.gov/sites/default/files/documents/reports/privacy-online-fair-information-practices-electronic-marketplace-federal-trade-commission-report/privacy2000text.pdf.

[4] See, for example, Hugo Teufel III, Chief Privacy Officer, "The Fair Information Practice Principles: Framework for Privacy Policy at the Department of Homeland Security," Memorandum Number 2008-01, (December 29, 2008), http://www.dhs.gov/xlibrary/assets/privacy/privacy_policyguide_2008-01.pdf; The White House, *Consumer Data Privacy in a Networked World: A Framework for Protecting Privacy and Promoting Innovation in the Global Digital Economy,* February 2012, http://www.whitehouse.gov/sites/default/files/privacy-final.pdf. The White House document also includes a comparison of interpretations of the principles by different organizations (Appendix A).

[5] One caution with respect to this interpretation is that some evidence from scientific research suggests that a sense of control may lead an individual to more readily disclose sensitive information, paradoxically increasing the risk that such information will be subject to misuse. Such a "control paradox" has also been found with respect to other behavior, such as safe driving (Laura Brandimarte, Alessandro Acquisti, and George Loewenstein, "Misplaced Confidences: Privacy and the Control Paradox," *Social Psychological and Personality Science* 4, no. 3 [April 15, 2013]: 340–47, http://spp.sagepub.com/content/early/2012/08/08/1948550612455931.abstract).

security. Cybersecurity can be a means of protecting against undesired surveillance of and gathering of data from an information system or network.

2. *Cybersecurity needs may sometimes conflict with protection of privacy.* Information that is shared to assist in cybersecurity efforts might sometimes contain personal information that at least some observers would regard as private. However, when aimed at potential sources of cyberattacks, such activities can also be useful to help effect cybersecurity. In addition, surveillance in the form of monitoring of information flow within a system can be an important component of cybersecurity. Generally, the risk of conflict arises from such monitoring, or in the sharing of information obtained via monitoring or surveillance.

Discussions about security should arguably distinguish between and address both aspects of the relationship. It may also be useful to point out that good security is not sufficient to ensure privacy. Individuals who make personal information available to others either intentionally or inadvertently lose control over that information, especially in the absence of clear and binding restrictions on its further dissemination or use.

That is something that neither children nor their parents may comprehend sufficiently to ensure that privacy is maintained, or, alternatively, they may be willing to surrender the privacy of at least some personal information in exchange for services or other benefits. According to a recent survey, most Americans believe that they have little control over the collection and use of their personal information by government and businesses, but most believe that is a concern that government should address.[6] There are many sources that describe the ways that information may be gathered and used, especially by businesses.[7]

Identifying information that is already available online can be difficult. Social media sites, email providers, and other service providers may make information on the data they have collected available upon request or through an online process.[8] Parents and children can use search engines to try to identify information available through them. Some companies also provide services to identify and help control access to personal information. However, information collected by data brokers and other businesses for data-mining or advertising purposes may not be available. Nevertheless, it may be possible to opt out of data-broker services.[9]

---

[6] Mary Madden, "Public Perceptions of Privacy and Security in the Post-Snowden Era," *Pew Research Center*, November 12, 2014, http://www.pewinternet.org/2014/11/12/public-privacy-perceptions/.

[7] See, for example, Federal Trade Commission, *Mobile Apps for Kids: Disclosures Still Not Making the Grade*, FTC Staff Report (Federal Trade Commission, December 10, 2012), https://www.ftc.gov/sites/default/files/documents/reports/mobile-apps-kids-disclosures-still-not-making-grade/121210mobilekidsappreport.pdf; Rebecca J. Rosen, "What Does the Consumer Data Industry Know About You?," *The Atlantic*, March 7, 2013, http://www.theatlantic.com/technology/archive/2013/03/what-does-the-consumer-data-industry-know-about-you/273829/; Steve Stecklow, "On the Web, Children Face Intensive Tracking," *Wall St. Journal*, September 17, 2010, http://online.wsj.com/article/SB10001424052748703904304575497903523187146.html?mod=rss_Today%27s_Most_Popular.

[8] See, for example, Help Center, "How Can I Download a Copy of My Facebook Data?," *Facebook*, 2015, https://www.facebook.com/help/302796099745838.

[9] Ken Gagne, "Doxxing Defense: Remove Your Personal Info from Data Brokers," *Computerworld*, November 20, 2014, http://www.computerworld.com/article/2849263/doxxing-defense-remove-your-personal-info-from-data-brokers.html.

Various steps can be taken to control access to personal information. Rules issued by the Federal Trade Commission (FTC) under the Children's Online Privacy Protection Act (COPPA) of 1998 set requirements for operators of websites and online services aimed at children under the age of 13 and those that knowingly collect, use, or disclose information on such children. Among other things, operators are forbidden from disclosing personal information about the child to third parties and must provide parents with access to the information and allow deletion of it.[10]

Some organizations have published broader guidance for how to manage the privacy of personal information online, both for adults and children.[11] An important component is to understand the provisions in the privacy statements and service agreements of any website operator or online service provider. The Department of Education has provided some guidelines that can be useful for identifying the implications of various provisions in those statements and agreements.[12]

In general, sources tend to recommend identification of such features and characteristics, and the importance of developing agreements between parents and children about what is and is not appropriate information to make available to others online. It appears to be widely recognized by professionals that absolute protection of privacy is not possible, or at least not practical, but that individuals can exert significant control over the risk of undesired access by others to personal information online.

---

[10] Federal Trade Commission, "Complying with COPPA: Frequently Asked Questions," July 16, 2014, https://www.ftc.gov/tips-advice/business-center/guidance/complying-coppa-frequently-asked-questions.

[11] See, for example, Privacy Rights Clearinghouse, "Children's Online Privacy: A Resource Guide for Parents," December 2014, https://www.privacyrights.org/childrens-online-privacy-a-resource-guide-for-parents; Privacy Rights Clearinghouse, "Social Networking Privacy: How to Be Safe, Secure and Social," February 2015, https://www.privacyrights.org/social-networking-privacy-how-be-safe-secure-and-social.

[12] Privacy Technical Assistance Center, "Protecting Student Privacy While Using Online Educational Services: Model Terms of Service," *U.S. Department of Education*, January 2015, http://ptac.ed.gov/sites/default/files/TOS_Guidance_Jan%202015_0.pdf.

Responses by Mr. Dean Garfield

**Information Technology
Industry Council**

**House Committee on Science, Space, and Technology
Subcommittee on Research and Technology
*"The Expanding Cyber Threat"***

Response of Mr. Dean Garfield, President and CEO, Information Technology Industry Council

Questions Submitted by Rep. Barbara Comstock, Chairwoman, Subcommittee on Research and Technology

1. How might U.S. industry be impacted if other countries do not adopt similar approaches to cybersecurity as the U.S.? How can we ensure that there will be a balance between legitimate risk reduction efforts and the ability of U.S. businesses to compete globally?

I appreciate your recognition that cyberspace is a global and interconnected system that spans national borders. Technologies are global, and threats do not stop at any borders. As a result, policymakers in both the U.S. and around the world should adopt globally workable cybersecurity policies.

The best thing the United States can do is to lead by example. Globally workable policies will enable all entities to best manage risks and preserve innovation- the latter bolsters our ability to compete globally. Here at home, we need to enact policies that are based on risk management, leverage industry initiatives and public-private partnerships, are flexible enough to allow entities to respond to constantly changing cyber threats, and encourage the use of industry-led, voluntary, globally accepted standards, best practices and assurance programs to promote security and interoperability. Other countries watch our cybersecurity policies carefully, and thus it is imperative that we show the right examples. If policies differ- such as by any governments mandating the use of particular technical standards or technologies—U.S. industry will be negatively impacted. Global approaches adopted by multiple countries allow each country to have access to the best cybersecurity products and services the global marketplace has to offer. When these principles are not adhered to by other countries, we sometimes see U.S. companies marginalized from business and opportunities worldwide, or making decisions, in the best interest of their companies, not to do business in countries where the costs of complying with non-globally compatible policies are too high.

2. Excellent security does not necessarily equate to privacy, it just means the data is safer. How do we ensure our discussions about security also incorporate privacy? Thinking especially about how often children and students are accessing networked information technology, how can parents really know what information is available online directly pertaining to their children? How can they work to secure and maintain the privacy of that information?

A number of laws address the privacy of student information as well as children's information. For example, the Federal Education Rights and Privacy Act (FERPA) includes privacy-related provisions applicable to student records. The Department of Education maintains a FERPA guide to parents, available on the Department's website, here:
http://www2.ed.gov/policy/gen/guid/fpco/ferpa/parents.html. Also, the Children's Online Privacy Protection Act, (COPPA) provides parents with certain controls over what information is collected about their children online. The Federal Trade Commission maintains a COPPA guide to parents, available on the FTC website, here: http://www.consumer.ftc.gov/articles/0031-protecting-your-childs-privacy-online

Information Technology Industry Council
1101 K St, NW Suite 610, Washington, D.C. 20005
t +1 (202) 737-8888, www.itic.org

Innovation. Insight. Influence.